T0353686

SIMPLE WINS

Stories from a Family Man

PHIL SIMPSON

WESTBOW
PRESS®
A DIVISION OF THOMAS NELSON
& ZONDERVAN

WestBow Press books may be ordered through booksellers or by contacting:

WestBow Press
A Division of Thomas Nelson & Zondervan
1663 Liberty Drive
Bloomington, IN 47403
www.westbowpress.com
844-714-3454

Cover Design by Abbey Foulcher

"Because He Lives" by William and Gloria Gaither
Capitol Cmg Paragon o/b/o Hanna Street Music
Copyright 1971

ISBN: 979-8-3850-3803-9 (sc)
ISBN: 979-8-3850-3804-6 (e)

Library of Congress Control Number: 2024924113

Print information available on the last page.

WestBow Press rev. date: 2/4/2025

CONTENTS

PREFACE

D uring my time as a Chaplain at Blackburn Primary School, I consistently wrote a column in the school newsletter. Dubbed the Chaplain's Corner, this was an opportunity to share some tips, reflections and a word of encouragement to the school community. After years of writing a weekly column, I had the idea to collect a few of these together and put them in one place. This was the genesis of "Simple Wins."

As I reviewed and edited my reflections in preparation for this book, I made the decision to add a Bible verse to each of the stories. This was not an option while writing a weekly reflection in a Government School. I initially debated whether or not to go down this path. However, the more I spoke to youth and young adults as well as many fully grown humans, the more I became convinced that the practical wisdom of the Bible is more relevant today than ever before. Regardless of whether or not you have chosen to embrace or explore Christian faith, the Bible provides a wonderful framework and a yardstick by which to make sound decisions, set priorities and gain insight. I maintain that biblical truths are as relevant and useful to everyone, regardless of where you sit on the issue of Christian faith. This is especially so if you are trying to raise a family.

I am super grateful for the encouragement, friendship and support that was shown to me over many years at Blackburn Primary School. While I could mention literally hundreds of names, I want to specifically acknowledge the three School Principals that I was fortunate to work with: Sue Barclay (nee Henderson), Clayton Sturzaker and Andrew Cock could not have been more supportive of the Chaplaincy program. They are wonderful human beings and they fully embraced every aspect of the program. Sue Barclay had the foresight to initially apply for Chaplaincy funding under the National School Chaplaincy Program. This was an initiative of the Australian Liberal Government in 2006. Initially Sue's idea to apply for funding was not universally embraced by everyone at Blackburn Primary. Despite this, Sue persisted with her application and secured the funding. Without much clarity about what the role would actually look like, she believed nonetheless that it would have a positive impact on the culture of the school. I was privileged to work with Sue until her retirement.

For better or worse, the subsequent Principals at Blackburn Primary School, (Clayton Sturzaker and Andrew Cock) inherited me. Despite not being part of my appointment, to my delight (and great relief), I was warmly embraced by both Clayton and Andrew. They immediately brought me into their confidence. They both actively included me in every aspect of the school community and publicly endorsed the Chaplaincy role to the parents, staff and students. I remain forever grateful for the collaboration, collegiality and personal friendships that I built over many years with these gifted educators. They remain great friends and I thoroughly enjoy any opportunity I have to reconnect with these amazing men.

Behind every school Principal is an amazing Assistant Principal. I had the privilege of working with three of the best. Over my time at BPS, I enjoyed wonderful relationships with Peter Dyer, Imogen Lippiatt and Marianne Fusillo. I learnt so much from these wonderful people in a range of different contexts. Each of them taught me something profound and unique about what it means to be a mentor, leader and friend. I got a chance to see first-hand how committed each of them was to making the school the best possible place to be for staff and students alike. Each of these leaders brought their own special flavour to this role. The role of Assistant Principal is not without its dramas. A big dose of wisdom, creativity and humour is essential for this role and Peter, Imogen and Marianne displayed these characteristics in spades. As at the writing of this book, Marianne continues to fulfill the role of Assistant Principal with great distinction. I am honoured to maintain a close friendship with Marianne and I enjoy our scheduled coffees. There are many other wonderful people that supported and encouraged me and the Chaplaincy program. The incredible Education Support workers (you know who you are), administrators, specialist teachers, parents, students and grandparents all brought something very special to the school community and to me personally. For all of this I say a hearty thank-you.

DEDICATION

This book is dedicated to my family. My wonderful wife Lara and my four amazing children, Hannah, Charlie, William and Gracie are a constant source of inspiration. Many of the stories and life events contained in this book centre around the activities and adventures of each of you. Thank-you for being such amazing companions on this journey of life. You've all made tremendous allowances for my many and varied rough edges. I value each of you more than I could ever express. God has been incredibly gracious to me in bringing you into my life. I look forward to many more years of family fun, beach holidays, snow trips, Beach Missions and lots of other local and overseas mission opportunities. I love doing life with you people. You are remarkable and dearly loved.

A big thanks also to Mum and Dad. You have been incredible parents and you modelled Christian parenting and Christian marriage for me in ways that were so natural, caring and instructive. Thanks for your many prayers and unceasing investment in me over so many decades. I have a rich store of memories for which I am eternally grateful. I have tried my best to raise my own family in the way that you raised me. You always did your very best to balance your commitment to mission and ministry with your care, sacrifice and dedication to your boys. Your sacrifices and selfless approach to life continue to inform and inspire generations of people.

This is a fun family snap taken in 2024 with our much-loved extras (Charlie's fiancé Ginger at the back and Hannah's boyfriend Jhon Jhon wearing the cap). We love our time together as a family and our family unit has been greatly enhanced by these beautiful extras!

STICKY SITUATION

There are some things you just never forget. They stick in your mind for all kinds of reasons. For me, the following incident was steeped in embarrassment. It was one of those moments when you want the earth to open up and swallow you. This involved my little Gracie. She's the youngest of my 4 kids and she's a young woman these days. This incident took place when she was still at Primary School. Prior to this incident, she had been awake for most of the night claiming to have some mysterious abdominal pain. She'd made a number of visits to our bedroom during the night. Each visit was accompanied with moans and groans. She was doubled over and claimed to be unable to sleep because of the pain. I did what every responsible parent does and consulted Google. The symptoms didn't seem to match anything sinister. Back to bed with some Dymadon.

Just to be cautious, we decided to keep her home from school. Of course, literally moments after the first school bell rang at 9.00 am, there seemed to be a Lazarus style recovery. We went to the Doctor nonetheless and watched a bit of television together at home. I had a conference with a client in the afternoon. I had scheduled the conference the week before (at which time I assumed I would be without a child). I had no option but to take the cute rascal with me to my office. This turned out to be one of the all-time professional low lights of my career. I gave Gracie some very strict instructions that she was to remain in either the adjoining office or in the boardroom. She was not to enter my office. I set about taking instructions from my client and his wife. He had engaged me to act on his behalf in his criminal proceeding in the Magistrates' Court. I was seated at my substantial leather-topped desk sitting opposite my client and his wife. I was attempting to look professional and engaged. Approximately 20 minutes into the conference, Gracie decided to give me a message. At any other moment in time, I would have gladly received a message from her.

On this occasion, however, the timing couldn't have been worse. Actually, it wasn't so much the timing as the way in which the message was delivered. Gracie found a long stick standing in a huge vase in the foyer. It was part of a funky decorative style arrangement outside my office. The stick was over 2 metres long. She'd pulled one of the sticks out of the oversized decorative vase. She'd then (without my knowledge) set about on a small project. She fossicked around the office and found some sticky-notes upon which she'd written a little message. She'd then skewered to the end of the stick her little yellow sticky note with the following message: "My tummy hurts, I love you." The stick was gradually poked into my office from the foyer. The client and his wife had their backs to it, but I had a perfect view.

While trying to sound intelligent, I could see the stick (and the sticky note) hovering within a couple of inches of the wife's left shoulder. Meanwhile, I'm desperately trying to appear calm and intelligent. The client's wife saw it first. It just about took out her left ear. When she noticed it in her peripheral vision, she was startled. Neither of them knew that I had my daughter sitting in the adjacent office and they certainly didn't expect a dancing sticky note to mysteriously appear in the middle of our conference. I did what I could to keep things together. Inside I was experiencing a mixture of embarrassment, disapproval and wild hilarity. Despite being quite cross, it was one of the funniest things I had seen in a long time. When the sticky note arrived directly under my nose, bobbing up and down on the end of the stick, I simply removed it and read the message. I then tried to get on with the conference as if things like this happened to me every day.

It's fair to say that our children give us our best and worst moments. You'll all be able to think of moments when you wanted the ground to open up and swallow you whole. These are the moments that we will all look back on and laugh about even if they don't seem too funny at the time.

We constantly talk to our kids about being resilient. I know I do. But we don't often turn our minds towards the levels of resilience that are required for parenting. They're huge. We need resilience in spades. Have a think about the aspects of your parenting that need a shot of resilience. Maybe it's your patience, your reactions and responses, your temper, or your approach to boundaries. Each of us needs to keep evaluating the way that we interact with our kids. Read books, talk to other parents, sign up for parenting courses and make it your business to be the best Mum, Dad, Grandparent or carer in the entire universe.

In Psalm 34, King David writes about a God that provides us with all the resources that we need. God is both our provider and our protector. He answers our prayers when we bring them before Him:

Psalm 34 v 4 – 10: *I prayed to the Lord, and he answered me. He freed me from all my fears. Those who look to him for help will be radiant with joy; no shadow of shame will darken their faces. In my desperation I prayed, and the Lord listened; he saved me from all my troubles. For the angel of the Lord is a guard; he surrounds and defends all who fear him. Taste and see that the Lord is good. Oh, the joys of those who take refuge in him! Fear the Lord, you his godly people, for those who fear him will have all they need. Even strong young lions sometimes go hungry, but those who trust in the Lord will lack no good thing.*

So, if you don't feel that you have the resources to deal with the issues that you are currently facing, ask for them. Take refuge in God and trust in Him. Imagine that, *"those who look to him for help will be radiant with joy."* Assurances don't get much better than that!

NO EGGS TODAY

For some years now my family have been fond of chooks. I had them as a kid growing up in suburban Melbourne. Chooks in the suburbs these days are seen as a bit kitsch. Back in the 1980's they were practical and a bit of a novelty. When Lara and I had kids, we thought it would be fun to get some chooks of our own. We've had a variety of shapes and sizes over the years. We started with some lovely speckled brown variety of unknown breeding. At some stage, we decided to update the flock and we bought a fancy breed of some description. I'm not sure what it was called, but we got this greenie/black chook from a special breeder. It was quite a pretty bird and this particular breed was supposed to be quite good at laying eggs.

In due course we introduced the new hen to its stable mates. I was told that you are best to do this at night time. You just put them on the perch when it's dark and when the chooks wake in the morning, they can't remember whether or not the "new" bird was there when they fell asleep. They just assume that they have always been friends and they pick up where they left off. I'm not sure about the scientific basis of this method of introduction. It's a bit like waking up in the morning, waving to your neighbours and wondering whether they are familiar or not. You wave, smile, shrug your shoulders and walk inside.

We fed and watered this hen for many weeks. It grew bigger and stronger and eventually began bossing around the other chooks. We kept feeding it and we waited with great anticipation for that first egg from this new bird. Sadly, that first egg never came. Instead at 5.52 am on a summer's morning in mid-January the "hen" let rip with a magnificent crow. It was crisp, clear and loud. Yep, SHE was a HE. "Elizabeth" was quite obviously delighted with his new-found talent. He crowed over and over despite our efforts to curb his enthusiasm. There's nothing like an energetic rooster to scuttle your popularity with the vaguely familiar neighbours. While we had become attached to

Elizabeth, we couldn't have him waking up the neighbours at the first hint of daybreak. So, with a degree of reluctance (more from the kids than us), we took him back from whence he came. We traded him on a couple of genuine egg-laying lady chooks.

It was somewhat inconvenient to chauffeur Elizabeth back to the chook farm in 30 plus degree heat. However, while we were in the hills, we found ourselves a park and a pool and we lingered for much of the afternoon. It went down as one of our most memorable day trips of those summer holidays. We hadn't planned an outing of this nature and we certainly wouldn't have been organised enough to plan such a trip at short notice. This all came about because of the need to grant the neighbourhood some early morning peace.

We all want the best for our kids and our family. We all want to love and feel loved. We all want to experience prosperity in one form or another. This doesn't necessarily mean material things. Often the things that we actually strive for are also very difficult to define. Words like connection, purpose and peace are all things that most of us would love to claim for our families and particularly our kids. There's no question that holidays, outings and impromptu excursions serve to build family unity and a strong sense of family identity.

Think about your own family. How many times have seemingly dreary tasks or otherwise quiet afternoons turned into fond family memories for one reason or another? We all desperately want our children to flourish and our family to prosper. This usually happens when we create the space in the calendar, prioritise family time, and look for beauty in unexpected places.

Psalm 144 v 12-14: *May our sons flourish in their youth like well-nurtured plants. May our daughters be like graceful pillars, carved to beautify a palace. May our barns be filled with crops of every kind. May the flocks in our fields multiply by the thousands, even tens of thousands, and may our oxen be loaded down with produce. May there be no enemy breaking through our walls, no going into captivity, no cries of alarm in our town squares. Yes, joyful are those who live like this! Joyful indeed are those whose God is the Lord.*

CALIFORNIA DREAMING

A few years ago, my younger brother Luke decided that it was time for a weekend away. Being the middle of three boys, I shared a bedroom for most of my pre-married life with one brother or the other. In fact, during the holidays we would often all camp in the one room for the majority of the school/Uni breaks. We did stacks together and we were each other's biggest fans. If one of us had a drama, we all had a drama. If someone had a project on the go, most of us became involved in one way or another. We all married, collected multiple kids and, as expected, have found ourselves pushed and pulled in all different directions for the last 25 years. The demands of home, family, sport and a range of wider commitments resulted in brotherly time taking a back seat. Before we all left home, we had a few days away together, but that was decades ago now.

It was definitely time for another weekend away. When Luke proposed a long-weekend activity, I admit to being a bit reluctant. It's not that I didn't want to go away with Andy and Luke. The reality is, however, that family life is busy and putting a line in the diary (especially on an official long weekend) has the capacity to create some logistical problems on the home front. We all (eventually) agreed it was a good idea. I was told very little about the arrangements. All I knew was that I needed to put a line through Saturday, Sunday and Monday. I thought that the destination might be somewhere reasonably local. At the absolute outside, I pictured a quick trip to the Gold Coast in Queensland (that's an easy two-hour flight from Melbourne). While the destination was not the purpose of the exercise, I was intrigued and a little unsettled when I was informed (about a month prior to the departure date) that I needed a passport. At that stage, it had been nearly 20 years since I had been overseas. I didn't possess a passport. I made an application and then waited by the letterbox. To the great relief of all concerned it turned up two days prior to our departure.

I packed my bag on Saturday morning (with no destination in mind) and chauffeured my brothers to the airport. We parked and grabbed our bags from the car, still oblivious to the proposed destination. None of us took very much in the way of luggage. A small bag each. What could you possibly need for a 3-night trip? It was in the airport carpark that I was told that we were going to Los Angeles, California. After picking myself up off the ground, I decided to ring Lara and the kids and tell them the news. Lara had bravely agreed to the idea of a weekend away without knowing the destination either.

To cut a long story short, in the space of 68 hours, we flew to LA and back, hired a car, spent a day at Universal Studios, took a tour of the Hollywood Hills, ate plenty of burgers, hit some shops, strolled along the Santa Monica Pier, spent a full day at Disneyland and I still managed to show up for work first thing Tuesday morning. It's probably the most hectic thing I've ever done, bearing in mind that a big trip for me is a road-trip to Portland, Victoria to visit my parents. A weekend trip to LA was totally outside my sphere of reality.

We met some amazing people, saw some spectacular sights, doubled our cholesterol readings and re-connected with each other in a profound way. We all discovered that even though life had changed for each of us in so many ways, none of us had actually changed much at all. It made me realise that strong friendships need more than occasional and ad-hoc conversations. I think that this is particularly so when family is involved. It is so easy to take close friends (and especially family) for granted. We spend our lives trying to balance our competing interests and priorities. While we may never have another experience like this again, it's a memory that I treasure. At the end of this trip, we all agreed to block out a night every six weeks or so in order to keep the momentum rolling.

To be honest, we haven't done very well at maintaining the momentum of this trip. Despite our best efforts, meaningful connection has been an on-going challenge as we each balance a wife, a swag of kids and respective work responsibilities. Nonetheless, I'm convinced that a strong memory bank of shared experiences can certainly assist to keep families more or less on the same page. While this is not a given, a good serving of grace, forgiveness and a genuine desire to keep no record of wrongs will give relationships the best chance of success and will help a relationship to weather the inevitable storms when they arise.

Think about people in your own life, be they friends or family, and make an assessment as to how things are going. If you get the feeling that a particular relationship should be travelling way better than it is, make whatever effort you can to re-establish the common ground that once existed. You may need to put on your cloak of humility and stop worrying about why the relationship derailed in the first place. This can start with a coffee. Of course, there are occasions when you may actually feel powerless to orchestrate change. Maybe things have been said or attitudes displayed that make recovery very difficult. This is a reality for some. In these circumstances, make it known that you remain committed to re-connecting should the opportunity ever arise. Sometimes, the passage of time can heal all manner of troubles. We should all be striving for harmony. The Bible asserts that harmony is as precious as anointing oil. Psalm 133 v 1 says:

How wonderful and pleasant it is when brothers live together in harmony!

That's the mandate. It's up to each of us to work out what this looks like in our own situation and setting. I'm not suggesting that it's going to be straightforward. In fact, the opposite is usually the case. But I'm convinced that we need to muster as much grace and forgiveness as we can in order to give our busted relationships the best chance of recovery.

BOOKS AND BOXES

One of the small luxuries that I have at my home is my study. When I first set it up, it had a certain "manly" quality. It had lots of shelves with leather bound books. Over the years, however, it has been occupied by the kids and their friends as they played on the computer. When they reached high school, they needed study space. Then Lara also moved in. What was once my precious "gentleman's lair" was overtaken by other people large and small. It also became a significant dumping ground for anything in the house that didn't have a specific place. While the kids play a role in this, I must also plead guilty to harbouring many, barely useful objects in my study. So, as I look around, it's now become completely swamped, mostly by stuff that is totally unrelated to study or work. Golf clubs for instance. For reasons unknown, there is always at least one set of golf clubs in my study – And they're rarely mine!

For a number of years, Lara talked about getting rid of my books. She was sick of the hundreds of leather-bound Law Reports dating back to 1865. She realized that I rarely (if ever) used them. She is a practical thinker and quite pragmatic. If they are not used, then they must go. I ignored these grand exclamations for many years. I regarded the Law Reports as the least of my worries. At least the books were on shelves and generally out of the way. If I either ignored the demands to move them, or vaguely agreed and then failed to formulate a strategy for their exit, the result was the same; my books would remain exactly where they were. But sadly, Lara was onto me!! She'd worked out my elaborate stalling strategy.

I arrived home one day and was confronted by a massive box of books on the floor of my study. Lara was actioning her plan. I never thought it would happen. I walked around the box for a week or two. Then I arrived home a couple of days later and three more boxes were stacked just inside the front door. That was four boxes in total. I took the hint. Whenever I left the house, she furiously started packing. My first reaction was to organise a "sit-in." I've seen these on the news and read about them in the paper. Perhaps I could just plonk on the floor of my study and refuse to move until she promised to halt her actions. A silent protest, however, seemed like too much work. I decided that I couldn't ignore the problem any longer. The pile of books on my floor meant that I was now forced to move them every time I wanted to open my filing cabinet. They turned into a real pain and I realised that I actually had to work out a strategy to deal with them. She's clever, my wife.

They became the proverbial elephant in the room. For so long, I ignored their presence. As they sat neatly on the shelf, I didn't think about the space they occupied or their lack of usefulness. The books were a bit of a hassle, but they were a hassle I could avoid because they didn't require any immediate action .....until they did. But then, they became a source of frustration. Lara had plans to give the study a major overhaul and my books were hindering this process. In my experience, most of us are excellent at avoiding real or potential problems simply because we can. We have things in our life that we know we should address. But instead, we manage to put them on the backburner and get on with the things that we understand and know how to solve.

It is, however, super important to name those things in life that require attention. Maybe it's your health or maybe it's an addiction. Maybe it's your attitude toward someone or something. Maybe it's your finances or a growing credit card debt. We don't need to try too hard to name the things in our life that cause stress, anxiety or drama. As painful as it is, I would challenge you to pull your own troubles off the shelf in order to work out how to solve them. While this may be easier said than done, the key is to formulate a strategy about what needs to happen and when. Maybe there are a number of things that need attention. That's ok. Write a list and start to prioritise. Not only will this help you to work out what you need to do, but it will also give you a sense of satisfaction as you tick off the items on your list.

The Bible has a thing or two to say about problems, challenges and difficulties. The Apostle Paul writes to the church in Rome and says the following in Romans 5 v 3-6:

We can rejoice, too, when we run into problems and trials, for we know that they help us develop endurance. And endurance develops strength of character, and character strengthens our confident hope of salvation. And this hope will not lead to disappointment. For we know how dearly God loves us. Because he has given us the Holy Spirit to fill our hearts with his love. When we were utterly helpless, Christ came at just the right time and died for us sinners.

As the boxes in my study grew in number, I was forced to relocate them. This was actually an incredibly important step towards getting things in my study (and my life) more organised. And while I miss the ambience of the 150-year-old leather bound books, their absence has revolutionised our study and created space for our family library. There's no time like the present to start sorting things out. While things will usually get worse before they get better, I'm convinced that the final result will be worth the hard work.

THE PRIDE AND JOY

Many years ago, when my lovely wife Lara was my lovely girlfriend, her parents lashed out and bought a beautiful new Ford Fairlane. It had all the bells and whistles. It was a special "Sportsman" edition with jazzy wheels and some "go fast" tweaks. Needless to say, it was their pride and joy. It cost a pretty penny back in the early 1990's. This maroon beauty sat majestically in the garage just waiting for its next outing. The "Sportsman" was often talked about in very hushed and reverent terms. For the first few months it was as if an important dignitary or Head of State had physically taken up residence in the garage, such was the excitement of the maroon beauty with the snowflake mag wheels.

I distinctly remember the day that I had to perform a logistical operation of some kind. I'm not sure whether I was picking something up or dropping something off at Lara's house. I had the trailer on the back of my car. I considered myself somewhat of an expert at backing the 6x4 trailer. I backed it up the driveway and then seized the opportunity to demonstrate to Lara just how impressive my backing prowess actually was. Her family garage was at a right-angle to their house. I backed the trailer up the driveway and then expertly angled it into the garage itself. I distinctly remember my final words before alighting from my car. I turned to Lara and said with more than a tinge of pride, "That's a beautiful piece of backing." That phrase has become folklore in our house. What I hadn't realised was that in keeping a careful eye on my right-hand mirror, I had unceremoniously backed my trailer straight into the side of the shiny new Fairlane. This was the worst possible atrocity that I could have inflicted upon Lara's parents. It was not going to bode well either for my longevity in the family.

I was instantly overwhelmed by the situation. I considered ending our relationship there and then and driving off at speed never to be seen again. It was a terrible moment and one that still haunts me. There were two things that I was extremely grateful for. First, the damage was minor. Second, Lara's Dad didn't know Karate. Change either of these details and things may have panned out very differently.

So where did I go wrong? I became so focused on my right-hand mirror that I took my eyes off the overall picture. In my determination to avoid a couple of old boxes and a bookshelf, I had damaged the item of real value. Have you ever done this? In life, it's very easy to be distracted by things that are actually of marginal value or limited importance. We get seduced by money or status or the expectations we place on ourselves, and in the process, we neglect and damage the things of real value. We are all guilty of losing perspective. It happens so easily. Things that actually don't matter can end up getting far more attention than the things that do. Consequently, we often don't give our family and friends the attention they deserve. It's so important to keep your eye on the bigger picture and the stuff of real value rather than the peripheral distractions.

My other major downfall was my sense of pride. I was cocky and confident. Both utterly misplaced. In hindsight, I took an unnecessary risk. I was showing off to my beloved and it backfired terribly. They say that pride comes before a fall. No matter how hard we all try, pride does have a nasty ability to creep into our lives. It can make for a very bumpy ride and it rarely, if ever, enhances the way we interact with others. It is so refreshing to meet someone who is genuinely humble. Humility is an extremely attractive and desirable character trait and one that is worth nurturing. It certainly comes easier to some than others. But it is definitely worth cultivating. Some people associate pride with power. In reality, genuine power rests with the humble.

If you keep your eyes open and your pride in check, you'll be well on the way to making some very sound choices. Don't get ahead of yourself and never think too much of yourself and your abilities.

The words of Jesus in Luke 14 v 11 say the following: *"For those who exalt themselves will be humbled, and those who humble themselves will be exalted."*

BEAUTY AND THE BEAST

Life in the Simpson household is pretty busy at times. Like most families, there are lots of activities that occupy our time. Sport, social, family, church and community events seem to dominate our horizon. I love all of these things, but they do take a toll. It's about balance and I'm not always brilliant at this. On one particular lazy afternoon, I found myself snoozing in a chair. I know I'm tired when I fall asleep in a lounge chair in the middle of the afternoon. This is what happened to me. In my broken slumber, I was vaguely conscious of my last-born Gracie fussing about in the lounge room. I was too tired to do anything about it. Over the period of 10 mins or so (I'm guessing), I got the benefit of a make-over. Glittery nail polish and some kind of coloured hair product. It was ultimately the hair product (purple in colour) that jolted me from my comfortable malaise.

For four days I sported my silver glitter nail polish. While it's all ok for weekend wear, I generally don't get around with any form of cosmetic beautification. A few people commented on it on Monday. Monday was one of my school days and nobody seemed to mind. I kept promising to do something about it. Turns out, it's not that easy to remove. On Tuesday I was out and about in the morning, but in the afternoon, I had a conference with a couple of clients. I donned the suit and tie and spiffed up the shoes. I tried my best to look as much like a Barrister as I could. Problem was, I was still adorned with glittery nail polish. I requested that Lovely Lara leave some nail polish remover on the table before she went to work. She did. But it was totally ineffective against the commercial grade glittery stuff that Gracie had applied.

With less than 30 minutes to go before my client conference, I was feeling the heat. What to do? And then I recalled that there was a new beauty salon around the corner. While I felt a bit self conscious, I dashed up, rang the bell and sheepishly blurted out my dilemma. With the response of a highly trained professional, the lovely Nicole moved into action. I was ushered in, seated and then the work began. She didn't miss a beat. She acted as if this is the type of thing that she encounters every other day. Maybe she does. Perhaps not so much from a blustering middle-aged man in a suit. Anyway, in a matter of moments, my nails were back to normal. It was so painless that I considered hanging around for a manicure. No time unfortunately. I rushed home, grabbed my bag and made the conference in the nick of time.

I felt bad that a lack of planning on my part had led to an emergency on behalf of my beautician (that's what she is now - my beautician). There will always be times when we need saving. While I try to keep these emergencies to an absolute minimum, it was so lovely to be the recipient of a gracious and caring spirit when my dilemma arose. It reminded me about how important it is to make yourself available when others are in need or distress. The next time that someone is in need of assistance, think about ways in which you can help. I love hearing stories about random acts of kindness and I'm sure we could all tell such a story. It's so important to ensure that we all play our part in looking out for each other and respond to the needs of others when we are able. Yes, it may sometimes involve some inconvenience, but it's a hallmark of genuine community. As we respond to the needs of those around us, we actually strengthen our ties with each other and we play a part in making our community a better place.

In the book of Romans, The Apostle Paul talks about the fact that our specific gifts are given to each of us by God and that we need to use them as best we can.

Romans 12 v 6-8: *In his grace, God has given us different gifts for doing certain things well. So if God has given you the ability to prophesy, speak out with as much faith as God has given you. If your gift is serving others, serve them well. If you are a teacher, teach well. If your gift is to encourage others, be encouraging. If it is giving, give generously. If God has given you leadership ability, take the responsibility seriously. And if you have a gift for showing kindness to others, do it gladly.*

This passage from Romans is a great reminder that no matter who you are or what you do, you have been given a gift, something that you're good at. In society, we tend to place higher priority on overt gifts. We admire and acknowledge those who are eloquent or funny or musical. There's no doubt that people with obvious gifts get more accolades. But the Apostle Paul reminds us that we all have different gifts. So, if you're a quiet achiever and you possess the less celebrated gifts, it's very important that you recognise how important these gifts are in God's great economy. Never stop using your gifts for the benefit of others and for God's Kingdom. Continue to teach, serve, encourage, lead and show generosity and kindness to others. In doing these things you will be playing the role for which you were designed. Relax and embrace the specific gifts that are yours and use them often.

BASKETBALL – THE NON-CONTACT SPORT

A number of years ago, our family decided to go on a Mission exposure trip to The Philippines. Lara actually singlehandedly organised this. I wasn't particularly keen on this as a destination. I suggested Disneyland, but Lara had her heart set on mission, outreach and service. I couldn't believe it! Imagine exposing all of us to such profound concepts when all I wanted was Mickey and Donald. She was super keen to get her head around the concept of faith in action. As usual, Lara got it right. It was a life-changing experience and we've been back many times since. We've also had the great privilege of introducing dozens of friends and family members to the same experience.

It's always an eye-opening time and a true privilege to meet so many interesting and wonderful people. Among other things, we've spent time in five Filipino prisons, we've spent precious time with orphaned, lost and abandoned children at a Children's Home and we've helped to feed the poorest of the poor in some very untidy conditions. It's a profound experience and one that has had a lasting impact on all that have taken part over the years. An experience like this certainly provides some much-needed perspective to our privileged lives.

On one particular trip in July 2018, we seized the opportunity to take in a bit of popular culture. To this end, we decided to book some tickets to watch The Australian Boomers Basketball team play The Philippines in the World Cup Qualifier at Philippine Arena. I'd never been to a professional basketball game prior to this. We thought this would be a great introduction. Needless to say, our little posse of 21 Australians was well and truly outnumbered. We did our best to support the Boomers amid a crowd of 15,000 or so very passionate Filipino fans. It was all in good fun, up until just before the end of the third quarter. The Boomers were leading their Filipino hosts 79-48, when things took an incredible turn. You may have seen the footage. It became an international talking point for those that follow basketball. In short, a massive brawl broke out. Punches, kicks and even chairs were thrown in the melee. And here I was, thinking that basketball was a non-contact sport.

There were a few tense moments for us as spectators. We were significantly outnumbered and we felt extremely vulnerable as we sat at the bottom of a packed stadium in a place where Australians had suddenly become quite unpopular. Fortunately for us, the Filipino spectators remained respectful and friendly toward the small minority of Boomers supporters. To our great relief, the crowd calmed down (the arrival of personnel in fatigues with guns and dogs may have helped) and we all managed to get out in one piece. My Brother-in-Law Rod was with us as was my mate Pete. Had things turned really bad, they were going to be part of my exit strategy. The diplomacy of Pete and the brute power of Rod were a compelling combination. This is not an experience that I want to relive in a big hurry.

My oldest boy Charlie plays basketball. He's small but fast. I love watching him play. While watching him at our local stadium, I noticed a big sign plastered on the wall. It read: "If you can't be positive then at least be quiet." If only this sign had made its way to the World Cup Qualifier in Manila! It may have saved some heartache for both teams and some associated diplomatic embarrassment.

It's not a bad slogan is it? Negativity, criticism and a loud mouth have probably got most of us into trouble at some stage. Most people struggle with interpersonal relationships on one level or another. From time to time, we all say things that we regret. Sometimes our mouths move faster than our brains. This type of behaviour inevitably creates disharmony and anxiety both within a family unit and also amongst friends and acquaintances. If you can relate to this, maybe the easiest thing to do when you find yourself in this space is to just keep your mouth closed. I accept that this is easier said than done.

We all like to have our say and I expect that most of us like to have the last say. It's normal human behaviour to want to espouse our own views and opinions. The trick is to do it in a way that is respectful, thoughtful and sensitive. So, if you find yourself getting wound up by a situation or an individual, sometimes it's best to just keep your views to yourself. Once you've regained composure and the heat has dissipated, it may then be time to voice your opinion in the right way and with the right attitude. In the New Testament, the book of James says some fantastic things about the power of the tongue.

James 1 v 19-21: *Understand this, my dear brothers and sisters; You must all be quick to listen, slow to speak, and slow to get angry. Human anger does not produce the righteousness God desires. So, get rid of all the filth and evil in your lives and humbly accept the word God has planted in your hearts, for it has the power to save your souls.*

Sometimes the older we get, the harder this stuff becomes. The key is to keep working on it.

A GIFT FROM ABOVE

A few years ago I heard about the recent discovery of a purebred Australian Alpine Dingo in Northern Victoria. Apparently, the Australian Alpine Dingo is somewhat of a rarity. They have been declining in numbers and are considered to be on the verge of extinction. Understandably, Dingo aficionados were super excited about the discovery. And while I'm pleased that the Australian Alpine Dingo population is now breathing a little easier, the thing that grabbed my attention was the method of discovery.

This little Dingo pup wasn't part of a special scientific tracking program. It wasn't being monitored by bearded scientists dressed in Khaki and clutching binoculars. It hadn't been captured on special infrared cameras hidden high in the Victorian Alps. Rather, and to the surprise and delight of everyone involved, it is believed to have been picked up and then subsequently dropped in a country back-yard by an eagle. An eagle! Are you serious? An eagle spies an endangered baby Alpine Dingo, grabs it in its massive claws and clumsily drops it unharmed in the backyard of some family home!! I have to say, what are the chances?! These kinds of discoveries are the type of thing that naturalists and other experts dream of. I think it's fair to say, however, that such gifts rarely arrive via this method of airmail.

Often in life, people talk about expecting the unexpected. This often has a negative connotation. Frequently when unexpected things happen, they can be negative or unwanted. Maybe someone gets sick or has some other misfortune or misadventure. Unexpected things usually take us by surprise and they can be very unsettling. However, we've all experienced very positive unexpected events. Things that we celebrate and look back on with great fondness. Things that make us smile unexpectedly. Things that change the course of our day, week or month. These are the things that keep us enthused and living with expectation for the future.

So, let me encourage everyone to live with a sense of expectation for the future. It's very easy to get bogged down by stuff. Family troubles, financial burdens, relationship difficulties, work dramas and ill-health. All these things are our reality at some time or another. They can cause us serious anxiety and they rob, steal and destroy our joy. But, if you try to live with a sense of expectation for the future, it may be that you'll be better equipped to see and identify the little highlights in your day. You'll start to notice the little things that go better than you expected; the "chance" meetings with friends or family, the unexpected connection with someone on the train, at the shops or at work. In our family, we call these little events "serendipitous moments." We love discussing them and comparing them and looking for the joy in them. Look for ways with your family or friends to build an awareness of "serendipitous moments." If you start adopting this language and culture, your kids and friends will start identifying these moments too. They are such fun when they happen, but they are sometimes easy to miss. Be on the lookout.

While you may not have a rare Alpine Dingo dropped in your back-yard, you don't have to look too far for a little blessing here or there. And when they happen, grab them with both hands, celebrate them and share them with your friends and family.

The Bible tells us that we should expect blessings and goodness from God. While life will always have its fair share of challenges, it's important to draw comfort and strength from the promises of the Bible. In his letter to Rome, the Apostle Paul says the following in Romans 8 v 28:

And we know that God causes everything to work together for the good of those who love God and are called according to his purpose for them.

So, be of good cheer and live life with the expectation that God wants the best for us in all that we do.

YOU DID WHAT?

O ur family often tries to get away each year for a little pre-Christmas adventure. Things are usually pretty quiet and it's a great time to unwind before the joy and madness of Christmas and the summer holidays arrive. We've been to multiple city hotels and also headed to the beach on some of these adventures. One year we packed up our happy van and set off for Phillip Island. It's a wonderful seaside destination and very popular with holidaymakers. It's about 90 minutes-drive from where we live in Melbourne. On this particular mini-break the weather was amazing as was the little seaside villa with a beautiful view over the beach and bay. It was just the tonic before cranking up for Christmas day and beyond.

My lovely wife Lara took care of most of the pre-trip arrangements. She organised our clothes and worked out what beach toys would make the journey. She made arrangements for our many and varied pets and she even gassed up the people mover. This made our exit from Melbourne much smoother than if I had been placed in charge of our departure. I was extremely grateful to Lara for her forward planning. Nothing, however, could have prepared me for one final detail that she imparted to me just as we pulled onto the Monash Freeway. As I was motoring along the Freeway, thinking happy thoughts about my mini-break, she casually informed me that she had inadvertently put unleaded petrol in our DIESEL van. WHAT? WHEN? HOW MUCH? ARE YOU SERIOUS? WHY DIDN'T YOU TELL ME AT HOME? Yes, the capital letters do indicate a slight rise in decibels. Not significant, but noticeable.

I loved my diesel van. It was comfortable and supremely practical. Not long after I got it, I had the diesel pump fully rebuilt. I just about needed to sell my firstborn to pay for it. So, I had this bouncing around in my head at the time that Lara broke this news to me. Now, I'm no diesel mechanic, but I was pretty sure that putting multiple litres of unleaded fuel into a diesel van wasn't going to enhance its performance or longevity.

As soon as Lara told me about her misdemeanour (I mean the very second) I detected a change in the van's performance. I instantly became acutely aware of all the noises and rattles. It seemed to be spluttering. Was it going to grind to a halt? Before filling it completely to the brim with the wrong fuel, Lara realised her mistake and then changed nozzles. She asked the man behind the counter at the servo and he said, "it should be fine." That was good enough for her. BUT HE'S NOT A MECHANIC! He was probably a 2nd year Economics student with little or no interest in cars or anything automotive for that matter. He was probably just doing his hours to fund his latest gaming console.

To cut a long story short, the van lived to fight another day. No permanent damage to report. If anything, it seemed to get slightly better mileage and it ran a bit cooler. Who'd have thought? To all the diesel owners out there, why don't you give it a go? Lara might actually be onto something. Or not! Perhaps send Lara an email before you try it and she can consult on the exact ratios required to boost the performance of your diesel car.

In my experience, it doesn't matter how organized you are, there are always things that pop up when you least expect them, things that you can't predict or plan for. That's just the way life is. It's right and proper to have a plan or two as you navigate through life. It's always good to write down your plans, goals and dreams if you haven't already. But, recognize that there might be the odd set-back or two. Try not to panic when they happen. Try to see them as just part and parcel of the bigger plan. There's so much about life that we can't control. Try to put your time and energy into the things that you can.

I've had a number of set-backs over the years that I could neither predict nor control. Sometimes these are minor, but other times they are earth shattering and will impact every single aspect of your lives in ways that you never anticipated. When these life-events strike, you can either give up and throw your hands in the air, or you can lean towards your creator and acknowledge your inability to solve the problem yourself. Thankfully, when I was recently blind-sided by an event in my own life,

I stumbled across some great advice from the Apostle Paul in his second letter to the Church in Corinth.

2 Corinthians 1 v 8-10: *We think you ought to know, dear brothers and sisters, about the trouble we went through in the province of Asia. We were crushed and overwhelmed beyond our ability to endure, and we thought we would never live through it. In fact, we expected to die. But as a result, we stopped relying on ourselves and learned to rely on God, who raises the dead. And he did rescue us from mortal danger, and he will rescue us again. We have placed our confidence in him, and he will continue to rescue us.*

These verses were a virtual lifesaver for me. Personal anguish, worry, stress and drama were suddenly put in perspective when I read these verses. It's funny how God speaks the right words at just the right time. Go God!!

THE GOOD OLD DAYS

O ver the years, my kids have always wanted to do stuff. When they were young, they always wanted to go somewhere or climb up something or jump their bike off some kind of structure. I have to confess that my initial reaction was often "NO" or "let me have a think about it." I didn't refuse such requests just because I could. It is often the case that I feared that these activities would ultimately end in tears. However, I sometimes feel bad when I think about the kinds of things that I was allowed to do as a kid.

I suspect that most parents do battle with this kind of thing every day. There are so many things that I'm sure we all did that we wouldn't even consider letting our own kids enjoy. Most of the stuff that I did as a kid now violates a host of local by-laws or State and Federal Acts.

One of my great joys was heading down to the incinerator. Like most houses, our incinerator was way down in the back corner of the yard. We would head out with a full box of matches and a massive basket of flammable and semi flammable material. These days, most of this stuff would now be placed in the recycle bin. But back in the 1970's and 80's we would burn everything. Paper, cardboard, plastic containers and even the odd glass jar. They were all thrown in. The more smoke the better. It was a very therapeutic experience. Of course, we didn't know any better back then. This was how every household disposed of its rubbish. There was no talk about global warming or carbon emissions in those days.

In fact, we were even able to do this at school. Two of the best jobs at primary school were the coveted incinerator and roof monitor jobs. The incinerator monitors got to burn all the paper and other flammable material that they could find, while the roof monitors got to climb on the roof with a rubbish bin and collect all the balls, bags and jumpers that had been tossed up there during the week. These days, teachers aren't even allowed on the roof with a "ladder licence." And forget any form of fire at school. The Fire Brigade would be on your doorstep at the hint of smoke. How times have changed.

Similarly, riding our push bikes around the neighbourhood was something that everyone did. Our only rule was that we were required to head home when the street lights came on. Mum and Dad usually had no idea where we were or what we were doing. No mobile phones or apps to check where we were. It's not that they didn't care; it was just what everybody did. Have bike, will travel.

Probably the greatest highlight, however, was going to the Nunawading tip. It was one of the biggest tips in our area. It was such a wonderful place. In the years before it was a neat hole in the ground, you could go out there and dump your broken stuff wherever you wanted. As kids, we thought this was marvellous. We usually brought home more stuff than we took. It was like going to a swap meet for hard rubbish: old mowers, busted bikes, car parts, furniture and home appliances. How times have changed. These days, kids under 16 aren't even allowed out of the car. They have to look longingly out the window. There's no chance of picking up good stuff even if you spot something in the hole. You just have to dream of what might have been.

Life has changed dramatically over the last 20-30 years. Our kids live in a much more sanitised world than we ever did. They don't get the opportunity to spread their wings the way that we did as youngsters. It doesn't mean they don't want to. It's just that things are so different now. As our kids got older, it actually became a bit of a challenge to even get the kids outside into the yard. Electronic gadgetry in particular, is a fierce competitor when it comes to outdoor activities.

So, while our kids are no longer allowed to burn rubbish in the backyard, or disappear until sunset, there are plenty of things they can and will do. It is important for us to let our kids be kids. They need to explore, climb, swing, ride, bounce and hide. They need to jump in puddles and slide in mud. We need to think about the good stuff that we did as kids and let them develop their own sense of fun and adventure. Not only will this help them to gain some independence but it will also help them keep fit and hopefully develop a love of the great outdoors. So next time your kids ask to do something a bit different, think hard about the reasons why you are tempted to say "NO." And I'll try and do the same.

I love the wonderful verses from the Old Testament book of Joshua:

Joshua 1 v 9: *This is my command – be strong and courageous! Do not be afraid or discouraged. For the Lord your God is with you wherever you go.*

So, there you have it, we are designed to be strong and courageous. I would also add adventurous to this list. Let's teach the kids in our life (be they nephews, nieces, students or our own children) this lesson by living it out for them all to see.

HANG 10

Can you think of something that you've always wanted to try but somehow you never got around to? Maybe you've sat back for years and observed others having fun and doing things that you'd always promised you were going to have a go at. Perhaps you hear stories or observe families or individuals who seem to live on the edge. I get quite unsettled by people who seem to just follow their dreams. Not because I don't think it's a good idea, but rather because I envy the courage of those who throw caution to the wind and have a go.

Most people have a list of things that they say they want to achieve before their time is up. I think it's a great idea to have a "bucket list." I'm beginning to realise though, that it is very easy to keep some dreams on the horizon without ever progressing them very far. I have a whole list of things that I want to do. While a number of them require money (and sometimes plenty of it), many of them just require setting aside some time. If you don't actively work towards your goals, then you are unlikely to find yourself achieving them.

It sounds simple doesn't it? Set a goal, put your head down and work towards it. However, I have discovered that it is dead easy to make excuses as to why those goals can wait. I'm too young; I'm too old; I'm not financially secure; It's not the done thing; I'll do it next year.

For years, I've talked about having a go at surfing and for years I've put it off. During the Christmas holidays a few years ago, I decided to finally have a go. I booked a surf lesson and off I went. When I arrived at the beach where the lessons were to take place, I discovered (to my dismay) that surf lessons are extremely popular with 12-year-old girls. Most of the other adults present were booking their kids in rather than signing up themselves. I felt a little silly at first, especially when I had to squeeze into an extremely snug wetsuit. I only just got it on (it was touch and go) and I almost needed the Jaws of Life to take it off again at the end of the lesson.

I found surfing to be much harder than it looked. Whenever I watch people on the big breaks, they make it look so effortless. While I managed to stand up, it will be a while before I catch my first tube. I was pleased that I took the time to have a go. I will try it again some day, but for the time being I am happy to have ticked it off my list. If I ran a surf school, I'd also provide a couple of sessions with an osteopath at the end. I'd be happy enough to build this into the price.

So, do you have a bucket list? If so, what things are on it? If not, why not? And what is stopping you from achieving your dreams? I need to make it abundantly clear that I do NOT pose these questions from a position of great strength or authority. I have got so many things that I want to do but haven't yet done. Of greater importance, however, are the things that you are actually managing to achieve rather than the long list of things that remain for the future. The key is to be actively working at your list.

Make time for both your personal and family dreams. Make them small and achievable as well as big, and brash. Don't be afraid to think outside the square. So, whether you are dreaming of the "Big Trip," the guitar lessons, the pottery classes, the renovation or just buying petrol for the mower, each step toward achieving your goal is an important one. So, what are you waiting for?

The Bible has a thing or two to say about procrastination. Proverbs offers lots of helpful tips on how to make your way through life. Proverbs 6 specifically addresses the urgency to free yourself from a poor decision. But I believe that the call to action that follows, applies equally to any human tendency to embrace inaction or mediocrity. Proverbs 6 v 4-11:

Don't put it off; do it now! Don't rest until you do. Save yourself like a gazelle escaping from a hunter, like a bird fleeing from a net. Take a lesson from the ants, you lazybones. Learn from their ways and become wise! Though they have no prince or governor or ruler to make them work, they labour hard all summer, gathering food for the winter. But you, lazybones, how long will you sleep? When will you wake up? A little extra sleep, a little more slumber, a little folding of the hands to rest – Then poverty will pounce on you like a bandit; scarcity will attack you like an armed robber.

This passage from Proverbs sounds a bit dramatic. But, there's lots of wisdom tucked away there. In short, GET ON WITH IT!

ANYONE SEEN THE KEYS?

'm not sure what things are like in your household, but I seem to spend a good portion of my day looking for the following items; my car keys, my glasses, my wallet and my diary.

Does that sound familiar to anyone else? I even have that disease where I will often walk around the house in a furious search for my phone while at the same time having a conversation on the very phone that I'm looking for. During 2020 our family experienced a full-blown car key crisis. When you drive your car every day, it's usually feasible to simply retrace your steps to try and locate where the keys may have been left. But during Covid, we drove our car very infrequently. So, when the time came to fire it up for the post lock-down school run, the keys were not immediately obvious (understatement). They were subsequently declared comprehensively lost. We searched in all the usual places; sports bags, school bags, golf bags, briefcases, discarded tracky dacks, jackets, draws, floors and seats. We also checked boxes, sock draws and even the shoe tub by the front door.

In a moment of clarity, I actually checked the car itself. I've been known to leave the keys in the ignition on countless occasions. Sadly, not there either. I contacted a Car Key Guy. His quote to replicate the key was enough for me to increase the household reward. After the last drive before the keys were lost, the car was parked awkwardly outside our neighbour's house. It obviously wasn't parked in anticipation of it remaining there for four months. I had an embarrassing moment when a new family moved in next door. Their 30-foot removalist truck arrived. They very politely requested me to move the car forward by a foot or two. Unfortunately, the car won't even roll forward without the keys in the ignition. I had to sheepishly explain this to my brand-new neighbour. This wasn't the greatest first impression.

It struck me that a car is of no use whatsoever without the ability to drive it. It doesn't matter how good or bad your car is, or what you think it might be worth. It doesn't matter whether it makes a statement or whether it's just transport. If you lose the keys, it's effectively useless. Keys and cars go together in a unique and extraordinary way. While physically a small piece of the puzzle, an ignition key is also one of the most important. Without it, you may as well buy a pushbike.

It got me thinking about what other things in life are rendered ineffective or useless because one element is broken or missing. You'll all be able to think of examples. From a relationship perspective, one of (if not the most) important ingredient is the ability to forgive and exercise grace. Grace is loosely defined as "undeserved favour." The ability to offer undeserved favour is a massive challenge. We all like being kind or generous to those who we like or to those that would do the same for us. But what about those that don't deserve it? These people present an uncomfortable challenge. How are we supposed to exercise grace and forgiveness toward those people who have wronged and hurt us? Those people that we don't even like!! I'm sure that most of us have a few names that come to mind.

Peaceful and meaningful human interaction will not survive or thrive without grace and forgiveness. Unlike the car without the keys, life will still go on without grace and forgiveness. But in my experience, it will lack richness, diversity and fulfillment if we don't grasp these important concepts. I should say (though it may be obvious) that grace and forgiveness don't come naturally. The world tells us to hold a grudge and protect ourselves at all cost.

Like anything in life, if you want to get better at something, you need to practice, practice, practice. We've all got people in our own lives who provide ample opportunity to flex the grace and forgiveness muscle. So, whether you're embroiled in a spat with a neighbour, a colleague, a partner, a business associate, a close friend or a family member, have a think about what you can do to change the outcome or direction of your current predicament. Be the one to find the keys and unlock the bitterness, anger and judgment that so often spoil meaningful relationships. You might not get it right, but it's definitely worth working on.

The Bible is packed full of stories and teachings about the importance of forgiveness. The book of Proverbs provides some great wisdom on the topic. Proverbs chapter 17 v 9 says:

Love prospers when a fault is forgiven, but dwelling on it separates close friends.

I should say that the keys were eventually found hiding at the bottom of a box at my work. By the time they were found, we'd already paid to have another one made. We've since lost the new set and we're back to one key again. Will we ever learn?

CHINESE DAY

I know what it's like to get kids out the door in the morning. It can be a very challenging exercise. While my two girls are usually self-sufficient, Charlie and William always keep me on my toes. On more occasions than I can count, William will emerge from the house eating his breakfast and holding his shoes. I hate being late to things and I'm embarrassed if I turn up well after the organised time. Despite varying levels of organisation, my boys have the capacity to exit the house in sub two minutes. They literally jump out of bed (eventually) and pull on whatever they can find on the floor and they're gone. While they always seem to make it, this method of departure does generate some fussing and stress. I grew up watching "Leave it to Beaver" and "The Brady Bunch." Things rarely (if ever) reached the red zone in either of those households. They never seemed to have any trouble getting out the door. No morning disagreements or differences of opinion. So, it came as quite a shock when my own noisy household started to take shape. I still sometimes wonder what a typical household looks like. I hope it looks a bit like mine, but I can't be 100% sure.

I'm sure that everyone can tell a story about the difficulties of getting everyone dispatched at the beginning of the day. I recall one occasion when my kids were young when we were feverishly preparing for Chinese Day. Our Primary School studied Chinese as a language. So, each year the school would dedicate a whole day to Chinese culture and games. This was always a major highlight on the Primary School calendar. It did, however, require high levels of last minute but intensive preparation.

In preparing for this particular Chinese Day, I was given strict instructions to search every nook and cranny of the garage to find the finest Chinese dress-ups and paraphernalia. This took some time. Boxes were searched and re-searched. It was like looking for the Tasmanian Tiger. People swore that they had spotted particular items, but everyone was extremely vague as to the whereabouts of these sightings. Chinese Day involved lots of traditional games, cooking and crafts. Lots of fun was always had. The obligatory donning of some form of traditional Chinese costume was obligatory.

To cut a long story short, on this particular day, the kids put on their Chinese costumes and prepared to head to school. One of the great highlights of the day was the costume parade. The kids would circle the gym dressed in their traditional Chinese finery. The distressing part of this story is that the Simpson family mucked up the date. We were exactly one week ahead of schedule for Chinese Day. I'm not sure how we got this wrong. Unfortunately, William made it all the way to school (on foot) before we realised our mistake. Charlie and Gracie were dressed in their oriental finery too. Going anywhere in fancy dress on the wrong day is always difficult to recover from. But there's something about painting your face and carrying an oversized oriental fan that seems to add an extra layer of complexity.

Charlie and Gracie were about to march out the door looking like a couple of tour guides from the Museum of Chinese History, when a neighbour arrived and queried why we looked the way we did. A quick re-read of the school newsletter confirmed that we'd got it wrong. William, who had left early, waited in a quiet place at school while I turned up with a change of clothes. It was all sorted with a minimum of fuss. The upside, of course, was that we were super prepared for when Chinese Day arrived the following week.

In families, things often don't go the way we plan them to. The best laid plans can turn to mud and even the most careful of preparations need to be jigged and re-jigged. I'm here to tell you that all of this is normal. It's often very frustrating when things don't go our way.

We have a concept of how we imagine things are going to turn out. Sometimes we just miss the mark, other times we miss it by a country mile. Perhaps our expectations are too high in the first place. The silver lining is that disappointments, scrambled plans and "catch-up footy" are both necessary and important in our development as parents and in the development of resilience and perseverance in our children. We all want resilient kids. Some kids are naturally more resilient than others. But without curve-balls, kids don't get a chance to develop these skills. None of us would wish disappointment or embarrassment on our children (or ourselves for that matter). But the fact is, it's sometimes unavoidable. Look for as many opportunities as you can to speak into these moments and remain positive when things do go wrong. This will go a long way to helping our kids to be positive, resourceful and resilient.

The Apostle Paul has a fair bit to say on this matter. For Paul, it was all about living the life that God had called him to live. And life for him was not particularly easy.

2 Corinthians 4 v 8-9: *We are pressed on every side by troubles, but we are not crushed. We are perplexed, but not driven to despair. We are hunted down, but never abandoned by God. We get knocked down, but we are not destroyed.*

This is such a great reminder isn't it? Even when we feel as though we are getting smashed from every side, there is always a reason to keep plodding and there is always a reason to look to the horizon. Regardless of our circumstances, the promises of God are that we are never abandoned and we are never destroyed.

BUYING A CADILLAC

Did I mention that my family was into cars?!? A number of years ago, Dad discovered the love of his life on eBay.com. It was a Goddess Gold 1956 Cadillac Sedan Deville. Winding back the clock, Dad was awestruck when, as a 12-year-old boy, he saw his first ever 1956 Cadillac at the Melbourne Motor Show. This started a life-long interest in these beautiful cars. The problem with the Cadillac that he spotted on eBay was that it was located in Tennessee! According to Google Maps this is 15,449 kilometres from Melbourne. This required some careful consideration: the major difficulty being that it is too expensive to travel to the US for a pre-purchase inspection. While you can organise people to carry out such things, this can be time consuming and also quite costly (most would say that it is much better to spend money on an inspection than to buy someone else's rust-bucket). Alas, no such inspection was undertaken.

After a couple of conversations with the vendor's neighbour (I'm not sure where the vendor was) the deal was sealed when Dad hit the "Buy it now" button. Dad has always had an impulsive streak in him. This has accounted for a range of spontaneous purchases over the years. It's a tried-and-true method with very few (if any) disasters over the years. However, the Caddy was a big purchase and, therefore, a big risk. For three or so months Dad wondered what on earth he had done. (I'm pretty sure he didn't share these thoughts with Mum). At the time that he bought this Caddy, Dad already had a white 1956 Cadillac. Mum didn't immediately see the need for him to buy another one. But, according to Dad, the new one was his dream car and the same spec as the one he'd spied at the Motor Show as a 12-year-old boy all those years earlier. The Cadillac eventually turned up in a shipping container in a far-off suburb on the western side of Melbourne.

My brother Luke and I drove across the Westgate Bridge armed with multiple sets of jumper leads, high octane spray and a few spanners.

We found the shipping yard and signed the delivery documents. The bloke from the shipping company then asked us how we were planning on getting the big Caddy home. He looked shocked when I said that I was planning to drive it. The thought of having it towed hadn't even entered my mind.

This big, beautiful car was sitting in a dusty warehouse. It was covered in months of Tennessee dirt and road grime but it fired up on the first crank. I must say that this was a great relief. It drove pretty well too. I recall driving it across the Westgate Bridge as I made my journey back to the eastern suburbs. It was a strange feeling sitting on the wrong side of the car. Left-hand-drive cars do take a bit of adjustment. It's pretty difficult going through the Maccas drive-through too. It all turned out OK. The big Caddy eventually found its way down to Portland, Victoria where Mum and Dad were living. Dad drives it for the occasional wedding and pulls it out on nice days to drive around town. It always attracts lots of attention. This transaction had a huge potential for disaster. But it worked out really well. As an aside, Dad's since discovered that his Caddy was originally sold new in Asheville, North Carolina. Classic.

The concept of buying items "sight unseen" is far more common now than it used to be. The growth of on-line shopping has meant that buyers and sellers from all over the globe can be connected in ways that nobody ever imagined. Covid has also made this far more common and acceptable than it used to be. It got me thinking about how this concept of buying something sight unseen can translate to our own families. When we buy something sight unseen, we buy it largely ignorant of its beauty and its blemishes.

When we commence upon the journey of family life, we are also mostly unaware of the beauty and blemishes that await us. Most of us would probably have some concept of what the perfect family should look like. I'm not sure about you, but my experience is that perfect families are a figment of the imagination. Family life is filled with imperfections, frustrations, irritations and disappointments and that's usually before breakfast! Hopefully these blemishes are also mingled with satisfaction, joy, delight, fun and a sense of achievement. The real challenge is to do our best to keep the balance between light and shade.

Concern or anxiety about the great unknowns of life are not a reason to avoid following your dreams or to walk away from wild ideas. Too many people miss their big opportunity because they are waiting for everything to be "just right." In my experience, there is never a perfect time for anything. We make our decisions, even the big ones, as best we can. Are we going to make mistakes – You betcha. But I love the simple advice of Ecclesiastes 11 v 4:

Farmers who wait for the perfect weather never plant. If they watch every cloud, they never harvest.

Sometimes, you just have to go for it!! Enjoy the journey and see what great lessons you learn along the way.

ADVENTURE, YES – RELAXING, NOT EVEN CLOSE!

I recall a time when our kids were much younger and Lara decided that the family should head into the city for a memorable night out. She's quite good at these adventures and has done them consistently over the years. These nights are always designed to build memories as a family. On this occasion, she booked a city hotel as a surprise and we all motored in with great anticipation. It was a fantastic idea and it was excitedly embraced by each family member. We struck a small snag when we arrived and were informed that the establishment didn't have any parking available. I dropped Lara and three of our four kids off in a loading zone with as much luggage as they could carry. My daughter Hannah (then only 7 years old) and I set off in search of an overnight car park. Approximately 30 minutes later we arrived at the hotel on foot (having walked over 1 km with a suitcase and a porta-cot). I must admit that I was feeling a little second-hand by this stage. But I was OK because I was picturing my palatial suite with the adjoining room for the kids. I was dearly looking forward to the peace and quiet.

Unfortunately, upon arrival I was greeted by the news that not only did the hotel NOT have any interconnecting rooms, BUT the only two rooms they could give us were Room 548 and Room 504. Yes, that's right, there were 44 rooms between us and the kids. As tempting as that sounded, we both agreed that it probably wouldn't win us a responsible parenting award. At this stage in our lives our 4 kids were aged between 7 and 1. We ended up stripping one of the beds in room 548 and dragging the mattress 44 rooms to the "honeymoon suite" where we threw it on the floor for Hannah. We managed to top-and-tail the boys on another mattress and we set up the porta-cot in the bathroom. This was not exactly what we had in mind and it was so far from the romantic escape we envisaged that it wasn't even funny.

The kids wrestled, raided the little milk capsules from the fridge, mucked around with the TV and jumped from bed to bed (not that this was a challenge since most of the floor was covered with mattresses and bedding!) I'm sure that we violated every possible fire and safety code. The change in circumstances had presented me with a choice. Either I could throw my hands up in frustration OR I could embrace this experience and view it as a memory building exercise. I must admit that I very nearly chose option number 1. It was a very serious internal battle.

I have slowly learnt that the success or failure of a particular event usually depends on what spin we choose to adopt. They say that attitude is everything. Attitude often plays a major role in the way we view our circumstances and surroundings. Sure, we didn't get much sleep and we certainly didn't get any peace and quiet, but by the time we checked out on Saturday morning we had walked along the Yarra River, been out for tea and breakfast together and inspected the Myer Christmas windows. These are memories that are now part of our family tapestry. Good memories.

Don't panic if things don't go exactly as you planned. When things begin to run off the rails (as they inevitably do from time to time), take a few deep breaths and try to salvage what you can from the unexpected curve balls. Ultimately, children are a magnificent gift from God. Even when things don't go as planned, it's important to remember that they are a great blessing. Sometimes, that's all that will get you through the tough times. Do your best to maintain an attitude of gratitude regarding your kids and love them no matter what. There's a great reminder of this truth in Psalm 127 v 3-5:

Children are a gift from the Lord; they are a reward from him. Children born to a young man are like arrows in a warrior's hands. How joyful is the man whose quiver is full of them!

FRIED ICE-CREAM

I remember the time when my kids heard about the ancient Chinese delicacy of fried ice-cream. I'm not sure how ancient it is and I don't know if it has its roots in China. However, the thought of deep frying something cold was an incredible novelty for the kids. They were desperate to try it. So, when we decided to check it out, we headed for Carrington Road in Box Hill. Box Hill, in the eastern suburbs of Melbourne, is an incredible place to eat. Chinese, Vietnamese, Korean, it's all there. It's the only place that we go for dumplings. What I discovered on this outing is that buying a dessert, without first buying a main meal in a Chinese restaurant is not the easiest thing to do. We knocked on lots of doors and perused a number of different menus. At one point, I was sent by the family to perform an inspection inside one of the more "traditional" restaurants. It checked out OK. Fried ice cream was on the menu and the price was right. What's even better, this place was prepared to set a table for 7 and skip straight to the dessert menu. Love this.

After such a long search, I was somewhat relieved and quite excited to share the news with the family. I made my way back through the busy establishment toward the front door. Upon attempting to exit, I promptly fell down the stairs. Sadly, for me, they were internal stairs. I would have coped much better had the extremely undignified fall happened outside the front door and into the street. Being internal stairs, all the tripping and subsequent falling was done in view of the patrons and staff. I picked myself up and hastily exited the restaurant.

A few moments later I had to take a few deep breaths, gather my brood, walk back inside and go straight back up the stairs that I had just fallen down. Being the only Caucasian male in the shop I did look a bit obvious. As I limped back through the shop with Lara, my four kids and a friend in tow, I pretended that nothing had happened. The bloke that fell down the stairs was obviously an entirely different bloke wearing a red cap. I felt a bit silly. I reassured myself that I had taken one for the team. In pursuit of this Eastern delicacy, I had made a sacrifice. I limped for a couple of weeks after this.

We all had a fantastic time as we sat in the Chinese restaurant and slurped away on our ancient delicacies. The kids were pleased with their treats and Lara and I were pleased because the kids weren't seated long enough to have an argument. Everybody kicked a goal. The only real downside was my dramatic exit earlier in the evening. It reminded me that most things in life that are worth their while usually have some level of associated heartache. In fact, everything that we achieve in life comes at a cost. Think back to what you have achieved. Your qualifications, your career, your family, your home, your friendships. All these things came at a price. Perhaps you are a gifted musician or sportsman. That came at a price. The challenge is to weigh up the sacrifice, the inconvenience and the pain against what it is you are hoping to achieve. Sometimes it's a "no brainer." Short term pain, long term gain. Other times, it's not so clear. It is sometimes easy to lose perspective without even knowing it.

In the Bible there are so many examples of wonderful people who managed to achieve great things, at a very great price. Very few of the remarkable biblical figures achieved anything without incurring significant cost. Abraham was called to leave his homeland; Joseph was disowned by his brothers and was thrown into prison; Elijah lived a nomadic existence and ran for his life; Daniel was turfed into a den of lions; Shadrach and Co were thrown into the furnace and Esther and Mordecai ran the gauntlet at the risk of their own lives. The list goes on and on. The Apostle Paul highlights his personal cost in a dramatic and blatant discourse in his second letter to the church in Corinth.

2 Corinthians 11 v 24-27: *Five different times the Jewish leaders gave me thirty-nine lashes. Three times I was beaten with rods. Once I was stoned. Three times I was shipwrecked. Once I spent a whole night and a day adrift at sea. I have travelled on many long journeys. I have faced danger from rivers and from robbers. I have faced danger from my own people, the Jews, as well as from the Gentiles. I have faced danger in the cities, in the deserts, and on the seas. And I have faced danger from men who claim to be believers but are*

not. I have worked hard and long, enduring many sleepless nights. I have been hungry and thirsty and have often gone without food. I have shivered in the cold, without enough clothing to keep me warm.

As the years rush by, have a think about the cost involved in what you are trying to achieve. While we all make sacrifices, it is unlikely that any of us have a list that rivals Paul's. But the point is, everything that is worthwhile takes a toll. Whether it's looking after your family, caring for a neighbour or friend, building your career or developing a ministry, you need to be mindful of the reality that true struggle is usually a constant companion. The key is to keep wrestling with it and keep trying to get the balance right as often as you can.

RUBY

I recall a time (in the distant past) when the Simpsons were in their pre-pet phase. Prior to having kids, we just had each other. No dog, no cat, no guinea pig, no chooks, no rabbit. Of course, children arrived and so did the animals. We've had so many that I've lost count. I recall when Lara and the kids started talking about getting a dog. There was a gradual surge of enthusiasm which reached a tidal wave that was simply too monstrous to hold back. Leading the charge was my darling Lara. Not wanting to be the bloke who dashed the hopes and dreams of my adoring family, I relented and the search began.

We spent many hours (probably hundreds) researching the appropriate dog for our family. We threw the net very wide and then gradually worked our way back. To cut a very long and painful story short, we ultimately ended up with a curious looking creature that basically ticked all of the boxes for the things that we wanted to avoid. It yaps and it sheds hair for a start. When people meet our dog, they wonder what on earth it is. Even the Vet was eager for a DNA test. It looks to me to be a Labrador X Corgi X Jack Russell X Dingo X Chihuahua. Needless to say, we didn't buy it from a well-known breeder. It's got a face that only a mother could love!

I would have to say that the most perplexing thing about little Ruby is the fact that she barks at everyone and everything. I watch her sometimes and she even seems to bark at the sky. I wonder what's going on in her tiny little doggy head. I suspect not much. A number of years ago, in sheer desperation, I rushed out and bought an anti-barking collar. $88.00 later, I was understandably eager for this device to achieve the desired result. It's designed to spray citronella in an upwards motion as soon as she barks.

The first bark was priceless. Poor Ruby barked and then all four paws left the ground in unison. Not dissimilar to a Harrier Jump Jet doing a vertical take-off manoeuvre. This thing even appeared to have some anti-gravity qualities. I was so excited that this menacing collar had cured one of Ruby's most profound character floors. It was shaping up to be the best $88.00 I'd ever spent. But then, she seemed to develop a taste for it. What dog enjoys citronella being sprayed up its nose? I was devastated that she regarded the spray as being a reasonable trade-off for barking at clouds, birds and the occasional cat.

I've met quite a few people that are just like Ruby. Instead of barking at the sky, they often say things that are hurtful, critical, unwise or just plain rude. We've all done it. I don't think any of us would struggle to think of a time when we blurted something out that we've instantly regretted. It happens all too easily. The sad thing is, that once we've said it, we can't take it back. I sometimes wonder what it would be like if there were citronella collars for humans. We could wear them to meetings or parties or even up to the shops. If you've got a teenager or an annoying mother-in-law, you might choose to leave it on indefinitely. As soon as you open your mouth to say something senseless, hurtful or critical, WHOOSH, a major shot of citronella straight up the nose. It would be embarrassing and uncomfortable but it might just save a friendship or protect a fragile connection with a family member.

Proverbs chapter 12 v 18 says the following: *The words of the reckless pierce like swords, but the tongue of the wise brings healing. (NIV)*

We all know people who seem to have a disconnect between their brain and their mouth. It happens. It's really important to work hard to be intentional with your words. Your words have the ability and the privilege to build people up and make them feel confident and loved. They also have the ability to bring hurt and destruction. Next time you're tossing up how to say something or indeed whether to say anything at all, spare a thought for the citronella collar. Would your words pass the spray test? If not, you may be wise to keep them to yourself. There are of course times when it's right to speak. Don't miss these opportunities either. But do it in a way that is dignified, gracious and constructive. That's the challenge for all of us, me included.

NAUGHTY NANA

A number of years ago my Mother-in-Law packed up all her gear and promptly moved to Mornington. It's a lovely seaside town overlooking Port Phillip Bay. It's about a 50-minute drive from our house. I'm not exactly sure what we did wrong. Clearly, she needed to spread her wings and explore her identity and fend for herself. It was a bit like waving good-bye to a teenager who was leaving the nest for the first time, but in reverse. Like doting parents, waving off their first teenager, we ensured that she had a good mobile phone and an iPad. We had done our job and now it was time to release her to the big wide world. From time to time, we wondered how she was getting on. She would ring occasionally. We wondered if she was making some new friends. Would she make wise decisions and avoid falling in with the wrong crowd? We hoped she would stay on the straight and narrow and not turn into a naughty Nana with too many choices and too much freedom. Those retirement villages can be quite a jungle for the uninitiated. I suppose we just had to trust her.

Now that I am so practiced at letting go, when my own children leave home, it will be a walk in the park. Anyway, Nana is getting along well: chatting over the fence, playing lawn bowls, drinking coffee and eating pastries. Why did we ever worry? Lara took to making a weekly trip to Mornington to visit Nana. I'm not sure if the draw card was Nana or the Mornington market. I suspect it's a mixture of both. We love it when Lara goes to the market. She returns with all manner of goodies. She's currently going through an organic phase. Organic everything: figs, eggs, cauliflower, beans, celery. It's costing me a fortune. The other day when I arrived home there was a massive tub of strawberries on the bench. They were big and juicy and bright red and no doubt quite expensive. The thing that caught my eye, however, was the sticker plastered on the top. It simply read "Slightly Imperfect."

In actual fact, this expression really sums up most things in life. Just about everything I own is, at best, slightly imperfect. Truth be known, I'd be delighted if my car, my house, my bike and my clothes were only slightly imperfect. They actually fall significantly shy of this standard. It doesn't mean, however, that I don't enjoy them. I like things that are slightly imperfect. I actually like stuff that is quite mediocre. That's just me. My briefcase is holding together with metres of sticky tape. I'm ok with that. I suspect that if we all stopped and looked around, we'd all have things in our lives that are slightly imperfect or worse. With a bit of creative thinking, most of us can deal with this eventuality.

As I gaze around my dinner table each evening, the rabble that is my family could also be plastered with the same sticker that was attached to the strawberries. Before we had kids, we always expected that our kids would be perfect. And to us they are. But with children come challenges. They rarely behave the way we want them to. We sometimes wonder which planet they came from. We all want our children to be perfect in health, outlook, physical appearance and physical capability. If they're not, we want to try and fix them. The fact is that our kids and the families that we've ended up with are a beautiful gift. Regardless of how they look, sound, act or behave they are ours and they are loved. We are all slightly imperfect in one way or another.

The magnificent thing about the strawberries that Lara bought at the Mornington market is that they taste amazing. Regardless of their imperfections, they never fail to deliver for the hungry hordes when they arrive. I'm working hard to accept my own rough edges together with those of Lara and the kids. I'm realising that slightly imperfect is an OK place to be. Rather than obsessing about how awesome everyone else seems to be, I'm trying to keep things in perspective and I'm enjoying my slightly imperfect existence. Psalm 128 is a great reminder of how valuable families are. Enjoy the blessing of your slightly imperfect family.

Psalm 128 v 1-4: *How joyful are those who fear the Lord – all who follow his ways! You will enjoy the fruit of your labour. How joyful and prosperous you will be! Your wife will be like a fruitful grapevine, flourishing within your home. Your children will be like vigorous young olive trees as they sit around your table. That is the Lord's blessing for those who fear him.*

THE LAND OF THE LONG
WHITE CLOUD

A good number of years ago, Lara and I went on a driving holiday around New Zealand. We scammed a car out of Lara's cousin Pete and toured New Zealand's North Island. It was a fantastic time sightseeing, lazing in thermal pools and eating massive choc-dipped ice-creams. New Zealand is an awesome place. While we were there, we stayed for a few days with the aforementioned Pete, his wife Andrea and their four kids in a place called Cambridge. It wasn't a particularly small town. It has a population of just over 15,000. It was certainly big enough to support a range of industries and local businesses.

Eager for some local treats, Lara and I dived into a local bakery to get some supplies for lunch. I requested a loaf of white bread. When the girl behind the counter produced a "block loaf" for my perusal, I told her it was perfect and could I please have it sliced into "sandwich?" She gave me a quizzical look and then with some hesitation she disappeared out the back. I wasn't sure what her issue was with my perfectly reasonable request.

She was gone for about 10 minutes and I wondered what on earth she could possibly be doing. I had witnessed those special slicing machines on many occasions and they only took a second or two. When the girl finally arrived back with my mangled loaf of sliced bread, I realized that this shop didn't have such a machine. The poor girl had been hand-slicing my fresh white loaf out the back somewhere. To say that my previously pristine white loaf was now squashed was an understatement. I can only imagine the nasty things she and her bakery colleagues must have been saying about me as she hacked away out the back. And while the thickness of the finished product looked a little more like "toast" thickness than "sandwich," slice, I wasn't about to complain.

When we relayed this story to our New Zealand family, they couldn't believe that we had made such an outrageous request. Hey, we assumed that the bakery had a slicing machine ok! As a result of our assumption, we also had a certain expectation. That is, that the white loaf would be returned in beautiful even slices. While the job was eventually delivered, things didn't turn out the way we had anticipated. There was a basic misunderstanding operating here. On the one hand, I couldn't work out why my request seemed so peculiar, while on the other, the unfortunate bakery girl couldn't work out why I'd made such a rash and unreasonable request. Had we actually understood each other, then I would happily have gone home and mangled the bread myself. Similarly, if she had communicated her predicament, it would have saved her ten precious minutes and I'd have been happy to mangle the loaf myself.

I'm sure we can all think of situations where we've made certain assumptions about a particular situation, event, person or circumstance. Similarly, I'm sure that most of us can also think of times when our assumptions were misplaced and our expectations remained unmet. Communication is the key to managing a situation like this. When we actually understand each other and manage to get on the same page, life is a whole lot more enjoyable for everyone.

Sadly, misunderstanding can be the beginning of the end for all kinds of relationships. Nobody jumps into a relationship or friendship with the expectation that it is going to end badly. And yet, so many of them do. The current divorce rates are testimony to the fact that many of us struggle to understand and be understood.

Relationships of every kind break for a variety of reasons. It often seems that very little can be done to save or patch up a busted relationship. Spouses, siblings, extended families and close friends often find themselves at war. It's sad, but it's a reality these days. Always be on the look-out for the things that unite rather than the things that divide. Try to find the common humanity that you still share with those who are distant or estranged. This may be the springboard you need to start putting the scattered pieces of a broken relationship back together.

Proverbs 20 v 3: *Avoiding a fight is a mark of honour; only fools insist on quarrelling.*

I sometimes wonder if the Cambridge Bakery ever decided to invest in a slicing machine. If so, I'd like to think that I played a small role in its move towards the 21st century. Thanks for the memories, Cambridge.

BIKE EDUCATION

During my time working as a school chaplain, I pounced upon the opportunity to undertake some further study. This particular course had a good mix of theory and practical work. It wasn't an MBA, a Masters or a PHD. It was, however, a course of great significance. It required utter commitment and even a sense of calling. And despite the rigorous nature of the course, failure was simply not an option. The qualification was destined to have a major impact on hundreds of people. This qualification put me in an elite category. Many people talk about this qualification but few are prepared to make the commitment to see it through. No, I haven't qualified as a Nurse, or a psychologist or even a teacher. But over a two-day period, I went and gained my accreditation as a Bike Education Instructor.

Over the course of two days, I learnt that the various bits and pieces on a bike actually have official names. I can't wait for the opportunity to start getting technical when I go to my next social function. I think I'll try and steer the conversation towards bikes and then just start to mention phrases like "group set," "front derailleur" or "chain suck." Provided the person I'm talking to doesn't know anything about bikes, everything will be ok.

During this course we rode around a basketball court and did plenty of figure 8's. We learnt how to stop and start and we had a quick refresher on basic road rules. We also played a number of bike related games. In order to spice up the training a bit we also had a race. I don't mean to gloat, but when it came to racing, I was the undisputed champion. I know what you're thinking: he doesn't look like he's built for speed. Well, you're right. I'm not. It was a slow race. We had to ride across the basketball court as slow as we possibly could. The loser was the winner if you know what I mean. It was all about slow and steady. As it turns out, I am much better at coming last than first when it comes to racing. And since this was the point of the exercise, I turned out to be the victor. Just call me tortoise.

This little race got me thinking about the concept of the last being first and the first being last. It's actually quite profound. Society these days is totally geared towards being the winner and coming first. You can't open a magazine or a newspaper or watch the TV without being told that the world revolves around YOU. Rarely do you see advertising or the media or glossy magazines espousing the values of service and putting others before yourself. I'm pretty sure that this stuff wouldn't sell papers and would be unlikely to form the basis of any advertising campaign. Who wants to come second? Who wants to put themselves out for others at the expense of themselves?

In posing these questions, I'm not talking about putting yourself out for your kids or even your parents or siblings. While this is important, I think we can all grasp the concept of looking after our own. But how often are we prepared to be inconvenienced for the sake of our neighbours, friends, colleagues or even complete strangers? This is probably the test. We are not going to get it right all the time. But I would encourage all of us to modify our gaze a bit and try to see the needs and concerns of others as being of utmost importance. Coming second can be a real blessing.

In the Bible, in the New Testament it talks quite a bit about what it means to serve others. In the book of Matthew, Jesus tells a story about some workers who were hired to work in a vineyard. He compares the actions and the reactions of those in the story to the Kingdom of Heaven. Ultimately, Jesus says, "So those who are last now, will be first then, and those who are first will be last" Matthew 20v16. Jesus goes on to give one of the greatest life-lessons a few verses later.

In Matthew 20 v 26(b)-28 Jesus says: *"Whoever wants to be a leader among you must be your servant, and whoever wants to be first among you must become your slave. For even the Son of Man came not to be served but to serve others and to give his life as a ransom for many."*

So, there you have it. Jesus himself talked lots about what it meant to be a servant. His radical teaching and selfless example of serving the least, the lost and the lonely continues to set the agenda for us over 2000 years later.

SKYLAB

The other day I found myself talking to my kids about space and the planets. I know very little about either. I learnt some interesting facts about how it all worked when I went to the planetarium at Science Works (this was another school excursion). I've learnt way more since going back to primary school as a Chaplain/adult than I did the first time around! I have since forgotten everything. Kids are generally interested in space. I sometimes wish I knew more about it all. The only thing of interest that I could contribute to the conversation about space was the demise of the infamous "Skylab." As a school boy in the 1970's, there's no way that I could escape the excitement of Skylab.

Skylab came crashing down to earth on the night of July 12 1979. It was an American space station that had been launched into orbit in 1973. I'm not sure what purpose it served. I just remember, as a primary school student, all the hype surrounding its re-entry into the earth's atmosphere. I was in Grade 2. The Americans with all their technology could not predict with any accuracy where it was going to land. It was, however, the source of much discussion. Time Magazine reported that Americans were holding Skylab parties and Skylab survival kits were being sold (complete with plastic helmets).

Until the final hours before its re-entry, NASA could only narrow down the possible crash site to an area covering 56% of the earth's surface. The statisticians predicted the chance of a person being hit by a piece of Skylab as being 1 in 152. A Californian radio station even offered a $10,000 prize to the first person to present them with an actual piece of Skylab.

Skylab entered the earth's atmosphere in Western Australia and bits and pieces of it were showered upon the town of Esperance. A 17-year-old lad from Western Australia heard the crashes and bangs. He later found a piece of Skylab on the roof of his backyard shed. How Australian! He immediately boarded a plane to the US and claimed his $10,000 prize. He became quite famous (for about 15 minutes) and came back to Australia with more than enough money for a brand-new Commodore.

It is fair to say that most of us live normal lives. We get up, feed the kids, make lunches, tidy out cupboards, pick up dirty clothes and pay the bills. These are all the important things that keep a household running. Others of us get up and head off to work in trains, trams, cars or vans. Life is very full. Most of us don't have the excitement of a "Skylab" experience very often. The youngster from Western Australia didn't plan his brush with fame or indeed his modest fortune. It simply happened upon him.

But I think that every family needs a "Skylab" experience every once in a while. A "Skylab" experience is an event of great excitement. It is an event that creates an atmosphere of anticipation and feverish discussion. It is an event that allows imaginations (young and old) to run wild. It is an event that motivates and maybe even inspires. It is something unique and even extraordinary. If we all waited for these events to simply present themselves, we may never share a "Skylab" experience with our family.

We need to be proactive in thinking about ways to engage our family or friends in these experiences. Maybe it's a BIG holiday or maybe it's a holiday construction project. It could be a trip to the zoo or a picnic at the park. Maybe it's designing a cubby or planning a fishing adventure to the local pier. Maybe it's a golf lesson, or a surf lesson, or an art class. It doesn't really matter what, where or how. The important thing is to take the time and effort to make it happen. Often the anticipation is just as much fun as the activity itself. God loves it when we celebrate and enjoy the blessings that flow from Him (and this includes our families). He also wants us to prosper in all that we do. Psalm 37 reminds us that God is desperately interested in each of usand that he wants us to succeed. So, look to God for every part of who you are and commit your job, your spouse, your children and your career to him.

Psalm 37 v 4-5 & 7: *Take delight in the Lord, and he will give you your heart's desires. Commit everything you do to the Lord. Trust Him, and he will help you.... v7: Be still in the presence of the Lord and wait patiently for him to act.*

VARIETY – IS IT THE SPICE OF YOUR LIFE?

I have to admit that when it comes to shopping, particularly grocery shopping, there are scores of things that I would rather do (and I suspect that this is the same for most). I have tried it over the years. Until recently, I hadn't done it enough to actually learn where everything is located. That changed when Lara started working full-time as a teacher. Suddenly, I began scouring the weekly catalogues and comparing prices on avocados and yoghurt. Despite having a bit more familiarity with the local supermarket, I can still find myself walking up and down each aisle scouring the shelves for a particular item.

To be honest, I find it hard to locate stuff in my own kitchen fridge. So, the supermarket presents a whole new level of difficulty. If I haven't found what I want by the time I reach the detergent aisle, I turn back and do it all again. I usually end up finding someone with a name tag and this makes life a whole lot easier. That said, I'm equally happy asking directions from an experienced looking mum-type. Seasoned shoppers are a great source of information.

A couple of years ago I had my first experience at a newish Supermarket chain. I couldn't believe what I found. There were the basic grocery items that you find in any supermarket. What impressed me about this one, was that you can load your trolley with the staples for the week and then buy a plasma TV or a pair of roller skates. Not so long back, I recall slipping into my local to get some cat food and I ended up with a 10,000,000-candle powered torch. The thing was massive. When Lara questioned the wisdom of the purchase, all I had to do was to ask her to consider how long it would actually take me to light 10,000,000 candles. I'm not sure that she quite embraced "big yellow" but I kept it nonetheless.

On another occasion I spied a petrol-powered generator. You never know when the lights might go out. I can hear what you're thinking: he's already got a 10,000,000 candle light torch. THEY ARE COMPLETELY DIFFERENT. On another visit, I spied a 9500-pound electric winch for the front of the car. While I'm not sure how it would look on the family wagon (and I have no use whatsoever for a winch), I was totally mesmerised by the winch and considered all the possible applications for my family. Sadly, there were none at all.

I suppose what I love about this store is the variety. You never quite know what treasures you will find. Similarly, you can go to buy something mundane (like groceries) and end up with something novel and exciting. This creates a sense of anticipation and this is what pulls me back there each time.

There is a life lesson tucked away in here somewhere. In our interactions with our family and friends, it is all too easy to embrace the mundane and settle for the mediocre; to just do what you have always done. Sometimes it is just easier to plod rather than run. Plodding is OK and there is always going to be a time for plodding. However, it is important to look for opportunities to keep life fresh and exciting. This can mean as little as changing a routine or doing something in a different way. In our family it can simply be a spontaneous decision to get "take away" instead of cooking or seeing a movie at short notice.

We were actually made for creativity and adventure. In the book of Genesis 1v27 it says that we are made in *"God's image."* Among other things, this means that we were made to think, feel and be creative. We have been equipped for adventure and joy, although some of us have forgotten this along the way. God has designed us and wants us to live with a smile.

Genesis 1 v 27: *So God created human beings in his own image. In the image of God he created them; male and female he created them.*

Imagine that, we are actually created in the image of God! It's profound and a bit overwhelming when you really think about it. And while life is never going to be a wall-to-wall celebration, there are plenty of things that each of us can do to ensure that variety and anticipation remain alive and well in our friendships and families. Have a think about what will work for you and your family and set about putting something into action.

FOOD PROCESSOR

The other day I was walking through my local shopping centre when I saw a shop that had published an apology about one of its products. The product in question was a fairly basic looking food processor. Apparently, it had been published in a catalogue with a vastly overstated power output. I don't know much about such things, so I jumped onto Google to have a look. The actual power output of the food processor in question was 250 watts. The claimed wattage in the brochure, however, was 2500. What's a zero between friends? I've since discovered that most electric chainsaws have a power output well under 2500 watts. Similarly, the Husqvarna K3000 Electric concrete cutter (14" Diamond blade not included) has a power output of 1800 watts.

While the misprint in the food processing catalogue may have been lost on most, there was, no doubt, a "tech head" somewhere in the community that had suddenly spilt their coffee over their junk mail when they read about the 2500-watt food processor. I suspect that they rang the outlet all day Sunday and then lined up out the front on Monday morning waiting for the doors to open. Oh, the possibilities of a 2500-watt food processor. Imagine the Bolognese sauces, the smoothies and the chick-pea dips that could be whipped up in a jiffy with this powerful unit. In actual fact, you could probably mash all three at the same time if you so desired. Even better, I'm sure that such a powerful device could be used on weekends to mulch tree branches and recycle hard rubbish. What a wonderfully versatile kitchen aid this would be.

Have you ever been sucked into something with the promise of vastly unrealistic results? Let's face it, we all love a deal. We all love something that seems too good to be true. I suspect that most of us, at some stage in our lives, have signed up for something or bought something on the promise that the return or the results would transform us physically, emotionally, financially or spiritually. How's that gym membership going? We all love to believe the incredible even when every ounce of us knows that what awaits us is probably a scam, a half-truth or just plain ridiculous. Late night TV seems to be over-saturated with such products. I recall the sheer adulation I felt the first time I laid eyes on my home gym. I was watching late-night telly when the info-mercial spoke to me. This home-gym promised abs, biceps and pecs that would see me having all my business shirts tailor made. Ok, things didn't work out quite the way I had planned. I still have it, and it mocks me from the corner of my shed.

There is a sense in which the thought of family life can be a bit like the 2500-watt food processor. We often see model-families in brochures and on TV, splashing around on sun-drenched beaches or taking a road trip with their beautiful children. They make everything look so easy and so much fun. Nobody ever gets car-sick while taking a family road trip when it's plastered on a tourism billboard. Imagine a billboard advertising a ski resort that displayed a set of parents scraping out a car seat and wiping a child down with a piece of newspaper!

Similarly, there are never any arguments or the need for parental discipline in the families that we see in magazines and on TV ads. Prior to jumping into married life, I didn't realise how challenging it could be to maintain a marriage, or how hard it is to be a parent. I think most of us jumped through the window into the lives we now have with a pretty limited grasp of what to expect. Family life certainly presents some hard times. If you've had a broken or challenging marriage, major dislocation with your children or unrelenting pressure on your family finances, you'll know exactly what I'm talking about.

For some, the disappointments can come close to outweighing the positives at times. The same could actually be said for adulthood generally. Responsibilities, obligations and expectations can take a toll on all of us. We need to keep evaluating how we are travelling with these things and try not to get overwhelmed by the task at hand. Don't try and deal with all your life issues on your own. We are designed to live in community and to lean on each other. This is particularly so when things are tough. If things are difficult, think carefully about who you can lean on. It's important to lean on someone. We all need that. If things are going OK at the moment, look out for those who aren't travelling so well and do all you can to be a support to those in your community who need a bit of a boost. If you're experiencing dark times, then reach out to somebody. Personal dramas are actually a part of life and we aren't supposed to solve these in isolation.

The words of Deuteronomy in the Old Testament should be an encouragement to you. In Deuteronomy chapter 31 Joshua becomes Israel's leader. Moses offered Joshua some wonderful words of encouragement:

Deuteronomy 31 v 7-8: *Then Moses called for Joshua, and as all Israel watched, he said to him, "Be strong and courageous! For you will lead these people into the land that the Lord swore to their ancestors he would give them....Do not be afraid or discouraged, for the Lord will personally go ahead of you. He will be with you; he will neither fail you or abandon you."*

So, there you have it. God has your back!! No matter what challenges you are facing, you can rest assured that you will not be facing these challenges on your own.

A FUNNY THING HAPPENED

've made previous references to my beloved diesel people mover. It was a Mitsubishi Delica. They weren't very common in Australia when we bought ours. They were imported from Japan and brought to Australia by private importers. We owned our van for a number of years and it was an awesome family van. I sometimes wish that I still had it.

There was one particular occasion when we took it to get serviced that stands out in my mind. We discovered a diesel mechanic who came highly recommended. The down-side was that he wasn't particularly local. His workshop was an easy drive, but getting home without a car was a bit of a drama. It was a case of having to find your own way home. Similarly, in order to pick the van up, you had to find your own way there. While the workshop did a good job, I didn't enjoy the logistical dramas.

For this particular service, Lara drove to the workshop. She took our two youngest William and Gracie with her. The mechanic then dropped her and the kids at the local railway station and they trained it back to our local station and they walked home from there. This apparently went quite smoothly. So, when the time came to pick the van up again in the afternoon, we seized the opportunity for an "all-in" family adventure. All six of us set off on foot to our local train station. Hannah and Charlie rode their scooters and William and Gracie hung off the pram (this was a while ago!) We missed one train as we wrestled with the ticket machine, but we were eventually on our way.

After getting off the train we converged on the local McDonalds (which is only a short walk from the station). I rang the mechanic who then came and picked me up. He drove me the 2 kilometres or so back to his workshop in Bayswater. Since he wasn't sure whether or not we would arrive before closing time he had taken the initiative of locking the keys in the car for us. This was very pro-active of him and a great safety measure. But unfortunately for me, I had left the spare set of keys back with Lara and the kids at Maccas. The mechanic was very obliging and was happy to drive me back to get them. We went back to Maccas, I got the keys and we were off again. When we arrived back at the workshop, I bid him farewell and he disappeared inside. It was at that point that I realised that the keys I had retrieved from Lara were actually the wrong keys.

When the mechanic emerged from the workshop again, I confessed that I still did not have the keys I needed. With a mild look of frustration in his eye, he agreed (for the third time) to drive to McDonalds, where Lara and the kids were still waiting. Upon arrival, there was some furious rummaging but all to no avail. We had left the spare keys at home. With a feeling of great frustration, I waved off our helpful mechanic and we settled down to order some Happy Meals (oh the irony!) I considered the whole experience a complete waste of time and I was frustrated beyond measure.

We walked back to the station to catch a train back home. By this time, it was dark and getting very cold. We walked and scootered home from the station. The whole process took around 3 hours. We had achieved absolutely nothing. Or so I thought.

While we sat on Boronia station waiting for our homeward train, the kids munched away on their nuggets and chips. Just for a joke (and out of sheer frustration), I posed the question to the kids: "Who wants to catch the train to Boronia McDonalds every Friday night?" Hands shot up in all directions. At that point my attitude towards this perceived disaster changed. I was forced for a moment to see things through the eyes of children. What to me had been an incredible waste of time, was for them a grand adventure. They wouldn't have had any more fun had we spent the day at SeaWorld!

Kids have the ability to see possibilities where we see problems. They have an incredible ability to find something interesting or exciting in things that we consider mundane. Without even meaning to, they often put a positive spin on things that can drive us wild. Perhaps if we all took some time to view things through the eyes of our children or grandchildren, our lives would not be so complex. Kids have the capacity to grasp complexities in ways that adults simply can't. Their lack of pretence and their innocence means that they tend to appreciate the good stuff without worrying too much about the details. They see things for what they are. Jesus said some truly radical things about children. They were radical then and they are radical now.

Matthew 18 v 1-4: *About that time the disciples came to Jesus and asked, "Who is the greatest in the Kingdom of Heaven?" Jesus called a little child to him and put the child among them. Then he said, "I tell you the truth, unless you turn from your sins and become like little children, you will never get into the Kingdom of Heaven. So anyone who becomes as humble as this little child is the greatest in the Kingdom of Heaven."*

So, next time things don't go the way you want them to, try looking at the situation through the eyes of your child. It may just save your day. If it doesn't, feel free to throw a massive tantrum! Not really, maybe try the time-out corner first.

DO YOU HAVE THE X FACTOR?

Like millions of Australians, I quite liked to watch the X-Factor when it was on TV. I'm not an avid watcher of television. I was, however, strangely drawn to the X-Factor and other shows like it. The Voice too. I love The Voice. With the X-Factor, it was the auditions that sucked me in initially. I could blame it on the kids. But I would often continue watching long after they were in bed. Perhaps it's just me desperately fighting the on-set of middle age. I love seeing people who have a spectacular talent, gift or skill. It's wonderful to watch.

I was relegated to "Business maths" when I was in year 10. This was a special stream of mathematics for those who were mathematically challenged. This class also happened to contain a reasonably high proportion of high-spirited personalities. We didn't learn much. Therefore, I can't comment on mathematical theory. I am, however, reliably informed (by Google) that in the world of mathematics, an "X-Factor" is *an unknown quantity which only becomes known after following a prescribed process.* In everyday life, we usually use the "X-Factor" expression when talking about celebrities, sports people or other high-profile individuals in the entertainment industry. The expression is also used to describe corporate gurus and success stories. I'm sure that most of us could probably comment on who has the X-Factor and who doesn't. It is, however, quite difficult to define exactly what X-Factor qualities actually are. I think this is the point. The X-Factor is a certain indefinable quality.

So, it's time to ask the question: Do you have the X-Factor? Well, obviously this is a very difficult question to answer. This is even more so when you're commenting on yourself. But I'd like to think that each of us has a bit of X-Factor about us. This doesn't mean that we're all good at everything we do. In fact, you may actually be quite mediocre at everything. You may sit and ponder exactly where your gifts, skills and talents lie. I don't think that any of this precludes you from having a little slice of X-Factor in your make-up. Remember that the X-Factor is an indefinable quality.

The other important thing to understand is that the whole world doesn't need to appreciate your own version of the X-Factor. It is enough that your partner or your children or some other significant individual appreciates your X-Factor from time to time. Your X-Factor may be your ability to bring a smile to their face, or your ability to make them feel appreciated. It may be the way you encourage someone or make people feel good about themselves. It may be your ability to invite people into your home and make them feel welcome. It may be the way that you generate enthusiasm among your friends and family for ideas that would otherwise seem mundane. I've got a good mate Cam, whose X-Factor is his ability to back a tandem trailer with a car full of screaming kids. He can back a boat, a jet-ski, a tandem, a car trailer or a 6x4 any time, any place, any conditions. He makes it look effortless. Are you getting the drift?

Let me encourage you to look for the X-Factor in those that you know. Appreciate and affirm them in the special things that they do and the way that they do them. Rest certain in the knowledge that you also possess rare and undefinable qualities. And even if your own (or somebody else's) rare and undefinable qualities are not immediately obvious, spend a few moments reflecting on the awesomeness of Psalm 139 v 13-18:

You made all the delicate, inner parts of my body and knit me together in my mother's womb. Thank you for making me so wonderfully complex! Your workmanship is marvelous – how well I know it. You watched me as I was being formed in utter seclusion, as I was woven together in the dark of the womb. You saw me before I was born. Every day of my life was recorded in your book. Every moment was laid out before a single day had passed. How precious are your thoughts about me Oh God. They cannot be numbered! I can't even count them; they outnumber the grains of sand! And when I wake up, you are still with me!

So, there you have it! This is how unique you are. God made you just the way you are and he's pretty proud of you. That alone gives each of us a bit of X-factor. Use your X- Factor to brighten the lives of those around you. And while most of us will never secure a record contract with Sony Music, win an Olympic medal or play in an AFL Premiership, your own journey is just as significant. Go YOU!

WHO'S YOUR CONTROL TOWER?

'm no aviation expert, but I love the concept of flying. The thought of going on a plane is always exciting for me. But, in reality, I'm a bit of a nervous flyer. I'm perfectly fine when the sky is blue and the air is calm and I can see the ground. I'm terrible when the turbulence starts and the plane rises and falls and bumps like a roller coaster. I generally close my eyes and practice my breathing exercises. It can be a challenge if it's a very long and bumpy flight. Usually, all I need is a bit of reassurance from the front of the plane. If it's bumping up and down without any explanation from the cockpit, I can't help but picture the ridiculous scenes from "Flying High" when the plane is being flown by the inflatable pilots.

My Father-in-Law was a commercial pilot for decades. He loved his job and he was very good at it. Back in the good old days, when aviation security was not what it is today, Lara and I were lucky enough to catch a ride with him from Melbourne to Darwin (via Adelaide). I managed to accompany him on the early morning pre-flight inspection. In the darkness of pre-dawn, with his torch in hand, he inspected the flaps and he actually kicked the tyres – I didn't know that this was even a thing. I certainly didn't think that an experienced Captain would physically inspect his jet plane prior to take-off.

On this particular adventure I was fortunate enough to find myself on the jump-seat behind him and the First Officer. Lara was content to eat carrot cake in her oversized seat at the pointy end of the plane. I was given a set of headphones and I was allowed to touch one switch. Whenever the cockpit door opened, I could see passengers craning their necks to see what I was doing. I looked very important in my civilian clothes. I made sure that every time the cockpit door opened, I was adjusting the one control that I had permission to touch. For all they knew, I was a prodigy flight engineer or a Check-Captain assessing the performance of my underling colleagues. The truth is, the single switch that I was permitted to touch was the volume control for my headphones.

I heard recently that over the course of an international flight, a plane is actually off course for 99% of the time. I have no idea whether or not this is true. But plenty of people seem to concur with this. The explanation for this, centres around factors such as turbulence, weather conditions and all kinds of other variables. So, while the destination doesn't change, the route between Point A and Point B will often look quite different. The pilots (so I'm told) will actually spend a great deal of their time during a flight making appropriate adjustments to ensure that they land where and when they are supposed to. This includes drawing on the experience of the First Officer, the Flight Engineers, control towers and other navigation aids. I assumed it was a simple case of set and forget. Apparently not. I apologise to pilots generally for my ignorance.

In a similar way, in our lives, we all have a starting point over which we have no control. And we all have a destination. We have plenty of control over the destination. It will, however, depend on a multitude of decisions in between. Some of those will be huge decisions that take a great deal of time, effort, thought and sometimes even prayer. Others are little decisions that can have both incidental or profound outcomes.

It's fair to say that our journey of life doesn't always seem to be heading in the direction that we would hope or anticipate. This can be true for us as individuals and families but it can also be true for us as a community. Sometimes stuff happens in our personal, family or community life that can seriously mess with our equilibrium. Sometimes they are blips on the radar that are easy to navigate while at other times they are full-scale disasters with traumatic consequences. Sometimes it seems as though the norm of our existence is actually the latter. When we experience on-going and consistent difficulty, challenge or trauma, it's easy to feel as though it will never pass. And even when it does, it feels as though it's just the eye of the storm before the cyclone hits again with even greater ferocity. This existence is very hard to accept or rationalise.

So, while there are no easy answers or quick fix solutions to these seasons, it's important to know that the storm will eventually pass and the sun will eventually shine again. It may not be tomorrow or the next day, but my experience is that the sun always manages to poke through the clouds again. Until this happens, it's important to keep making the necessary adjustments. Keep looking for familiar reference points, keep your eyes on your surroundings, maintain your gaze on the horizon and your destination. Keep your lines of communication open and speak to others who can help to guide and advise on suggested ways of getting you through the rough patches. Identify who are the Captains, First Officers, Flight Engineers or Control Towers in your world and rely on them for guidance, direction, and reassurance. Remember that all of these aids are designed to help you. Without them, the consequences can be catastrophic.

There are plenty of people who can point you in the right direction. Just make sure you ask. Sometimes, it's only the Godly wisdom of others and your faith in a God who can perform miracles that will help to keep you on track or bring you back on track should you lose your way.

Proverbs 3 v 5-6: *Trust in the Lord with all your heart; and lean not on your own understanding; in all your ways submit to him, and he will make your paths straight. (NIV)*

AROUND THE BAY IN A DAY

A number of years ago I had the idea that I would like to join the masses and have a go at riding "Around the Bay in a Day." This is a cycling event that starts in Melbourne and finishes in Melbourne. The event follows the road network that circumnavigates Port Phillip Bay. All up, it's about 210 km. It takes in all manner of scenery and even includes a ferry crossing from Sorrento to Queenscliff. Not only is the ferry trip very scenic, but it's also a nice respite from sitting on the bike seat. So, I and some similarly proportioned friends, decided this would be a challenge worth committing some time to. Having successfully participated in the "Bike-education" program at school (which included multiple laps of the basketball courts and a few laps of the block), I felt that I was ready to take my cycling to the next level.

I jumped on-line and filled in all the necessary boxes to enable me to register. I knew that if I committed my VISA details, there would be an added incentive to get out and have a go. Before I finalised my registration, I also bought some "Around the Bay" merchandise. I lashed out and ordered a cycling cap. It wasn't too expensive and I thought that I would probably get some good use out of it. It arrived in the mail. Unfortunately, it is one of those funny little ones that you see people wearing on the Tour de France (it is a cycling cap after all). I looked like I should have been on the album cover of a new Boy band CD. It's still in pristine condition. I simply wasn't prepared to wear it in public.

In preparation for this event, I accepted an invitation to join some semi-serious cycling enthusiast on a training ride. It was pretty messy. I found it far more challenging than the bike-ed program (that may come as no surprise). These guys just take off and ride fast. When they get to big hills, they seem to speed up. Some of them even seem to smile. All I wanted to do was get off and walk. On both occasions that I joined them, we stopped for breakfast. I watched as they ate bacon and eggs and toast. If I were to order such a "snack," I would need to find the closest railway station. Riding home simply wouldn't be an option.

Prior to one particular training ride, it was announced that we were riding to Station Pier in Port Melbourne. This was about 25 km away. They thought I was joking when I asked how we were going to get home. Anyway, we got there - and back. I was feeling pretty sore by the time I got home. Modest inclines that I don't even notice in my car seemed to appear from nowhere. At one point, I had no choice but to get off and walk up the Barkers Road hill. It always looks bad when a middle-aged man in Lycra is seen pushing his bike up a hill. It was either get off and walk or call a MICA Ambulance.

When I drive my car, I get terribly frustrated when I keep getting stopped at red lights. Red lights are a necessary inconvenience. We all know that without them, driving would be a very dangerous affair. When out riding with my merry band of cyclists, however, I developed a whole new appreciation for red lights. You see, when you sit off the back of a "bunch" (that's a bit of cycling talk) and the bunch disappears over the horizon, a red light can be your best friend. Not only does it give you a chance to keep the bunch within sight but it also enables a scheduled rest break. So instead of having to suffer the indignity of yelling out for a break, I just smile to myself when the red lights halt the momentum. The longer the red light the better.

My short-lived brush with cycling has taught me that inconvenience is really all about perspective. When inconvenience presents itself, we have the power to choose how we react to it. Either we can get frustrated and even lose our temper or we can see the inconvenience for what it is and even make the most out of it. So, whether it's a red light or a green light, on so many levels, cycling provides lots of helpful metaphors for life. Ups and downs, coasting and struggling, stops and starts, perseverance, rhythm, communication and the power of the peloton to drag you home are all an important part of cycling. They will keep you on track and moving in the right direction towards your ultimate goal. In the book of Philippians, the Apostle Paul has something remarkable to say about pressing on. In Philippians 3 v 12(b)-14 he says:

But I press on to possess that perfection for which Christ Jesus first possessed me. No, dear brothers and sisters, I have not achieved it, but I focus on this one thing. Forgetting the past and looking forward to what lies ahead, I press on to reach the end of the race and receive the heavenly prize for which God, through Christ Jesus, is calling us.

PRECISION DRIVING

Things are a bit different in the Simpson family these days. We now have multiple drivers. I recall the emotion of when our eldest daughter Hannah got her L plates. It was a mix of fear and excitement (fear for me and excitement for her). After a few laps of the local shops and the odd back-street drive, she then did very little driving over the following 12 months. As time ticked by, we all decided that we needed to get some much-needed hours under the belt. She needed 120 hours of supervised driving before she could sit her licence test. As my son Charlie was soon to get his L plates as well, I wanted to avoid too much competition for the driver's seat. To this end, we set off on our Easter holiday to Portland with L plates attached and Hannah at the wheel. I'd like to say that I felt like Elvis being chauffeured around. Although, I suspect that Elvis was quite relaxed while being driven from place to place. The same wasn't the case for me. Mine was more nervous tension mixed with a touch of high-level anxiety.

Anyway, my parents live on a small farm about 10 minutes-drive out of Portland. Portland is a lovely seaside town about 5 hours south-west of Melbourne. The roads around their little farm are a great place to get some hours up. The farm itself has a big horseshoe driveway. But, if there's a car in the way, the only option is to reverse out the same way that you enter. It has a reasonably long driveway (much longer than a house in the suburbs) and can be a little tricky to reverse out of. I explained this to Hannah. I then used this as a teaching opportunity. As in, "this is pretty much how it's done. Watch and learn." I'm sure you all get the drift of my advanced instructional techniques. The problem, however, was that in my enthusiasm to impart this lesson, I backed the family car into my Dad's letterbox. I genuinely couldn't believe it. The pesky thing was hiding behind a bush and literally jumped out at the last moment. The letterbox was damaged (not beyond repair), the car was fine, my pride was a write-off. I simply couldn't believe it.

My Dad helpfully advised me that in over 10 years, nobody else had managed such a feat. I'm still wondering if that was offered by way of encouragement, empathy or simple observation. Regardless, my attempted object lesson to Hannah came right back at me. So, what did I learn?

- *It's always dangerous to tout yourself as an expert – Because pride usually comes before a fall*
- *It's ok to let others make mistakes – That's generally how they learn*
- *Never be too hard or critical of the actions of others – Chances are that you may not be able to do much better yourself*

Of course, my attitude was adjusted by this little episode. And while there are still times when "Dad knows best," this incident demonstrated that I needed to loosen my grip a bit (possibly quite a lot) when it comes to the freedoms and decision making of my kids. This is a monster challenge for every parent. Sadly, as a Barrister, I constantly meet parents who continue to make excuses for their precious children.

Many parents speak for them, excuse their behaviour and they pamper them to an absurd degree. While a bit of this is inevitable, I'm bemused by how often I see it played out by parents towards children in their 20's and 30's. My assessment is that the over-protective parent ends up with a child who simply never grows up. I think that the reason that we find it so hard to let go, is that we worry about what might become of our darling children if we don't micromanage them. The Bible says plenty about worry. Specifically, we're told not to worry.

In the New Testament, the book of Luke says the following in Luke 12 v 22-26:

Then, turning to his disciples, Jesus said, "That is why I tell you not to worry about everyday life – whether you have enough food to eat or enough clothes to wear. For life is more than food, and your body more than clothing. Look at the ravens. They don't plant or harvest or store food in barns, for God feeds them. And you are far more valuable to him than any birds! Can all your worries add a single moment to your life? And if worry can't accomplish a little thing like that, what's the use of worrying over bigger things?"

So, there you have it: If God cares for the ravens, he's going to care for the stuff that really matters to each of us. Jesus wants us to give up the art of worrying. When it comes to our kids, work out when it's time to let out some rope. No need to throw the leash out altogether. That will create other (possibly worse) problems. Keep the communication up, read some books, talk to parents who have done the journey and stay creative.

LIMO DRIVER

've never had a ride in a limo, but I've always been keen. I've just never really had the occasion. I love the look of the big stretch Hummers that cruise around the place. I got up close and personal with one in Sydney a few years ago. It was parked outside a flash hotel in the suburb of Manly and I managed a sticky beak. My daughter Hannah got to ride in one for her school formal. I stuck my head in that one as well. But that's as far as I've ever been. Limos are certainly more common these days than they were when I was a kid. Usually reserved for school formals, weddings, hens' nights and funerals, people like to mark significant occasions with big, jazzy transportation. When you book a jazzy car, the expectation is that a jazzy car will turn up.

One morning on the way to work, I was sitting in peak hour traffic when I saw a classic sight. Sitting right beside me in the traffic was an old silver Ford LTD. This thing was probably mid 1980's. This old workhorse had seen better days and had clearly been around the block a few times. It hadn't been washed in about 5 years or so. It had significant accident damage on the front right-hand side and it was missing the panel under the bumper bar. In keeping with the great Australian tradition, the radio antenna had been snapped off and replaced with the iconic metal coat hanger. In short, it looked as if it was on its way to the scrap metal shop.

We've all seen cars like this around. I've spent around 20 of the last 25 years driving cars just like this. They have a great deal of appeal to me, especially if they're cheap. What amused me about this one, was that sitting proudly in the driver's seat was a distinguished looking man, wearing a Chauffeur's cap, and a waistcoat. What amused me even more was that this silver LTD had a woman sitting in the back seat as if it was the most normal thing in the world. Presumably she was off to some high-flying board meeting in the Paris end of Collins Street.

It instantly got me thinking about a couple of things. Firstly, how would I react if I'd ordered a Limo Service and this old machine turned up (coat hanger and all?) This wasn't just a silver LTD in need of a cut and polish. It was a genuine pile of junk. I'll be honest and say that I'd be a bit deflated (and a bit intrigued). That said, the ageing Ford had a certain classic charm. I'm not sure that every high-flying executive would see it that way. Further, I loved the fact that the dignified man piloting the Ford LTD looked as though he could have been driving Beyonce to the Grammys in a million dollar stretch Hummer. Both the chauffeur and passenger looked completely at home as they crept along in the peak hour rush.

There are a couple of great lessons in this visual. In life, you don't always get what you bargained for. We have the image in our mind about how things should look. Most of us want things that are big, shiny and flashy. However, reality dictates that we end up with things that are slightly battered and dinged and in need of a bit of spit and polish. The key is to adjust your thinking and learn to appreciate the different twists and turns that come our way. I have spoken to many people over the years who have had to adjust their gaze for one reason or another. It isn't impossible to find great richness and fulfillment even though things don't look the way we imagined. Similarly, while circumstances are often beyond our control, attitude is most definitely a choice. Even if we're wearing a cap and waistcoat and proudly driving something well beyond its use-by date, we can all choose to make the best of what we've got.

I love the words of the Apostle Paul to the Philippians about contentment.

Philippians 4 v 11-13 says the following:

Not that I was ever in need, for I have learned how to be content with whatever I have. I know how to live on almost nothing or with everything. I have learned the secret of living in every situation, whether it is with a full stomach or empty, with plenty or little. For I can do all things through Christ who gives me strength.

If the Apostle Paul was living in our times, I'm pretty sure that he wouldn't have cared if an ancient Ford LTD had picked him up. I get the impression that he would express gratitude for the ride and enjoy the experience. Think about what it means to re-discover the lost art of contentment. It's not easy these days. If we view everything as a gift from God, this is likely to increase our gratitude and hopefully increase our feelings of contentment for our present circumstances.

BAMBOO – A LESSON IN LIFE

A couple of years ago, I waved off my daughter Hannah as she made her way to her Year 12 English Exam. There is a sense in which 13 years of schooling had culminated in this one moment. I still remember with absolute clarity her very first day of primary school. Lara and I walked her to school and gave her a big hug as we knelt on the tan-bark under the shadows of the big yellow slide. This was moments before she made her way to her first ever classroom. Yes, it was a long time ago, but it feels like yesterday. Back then, I waved good-bye with a heavy heart. This time around it was with mixed emotions. For her sake (and for the well-being of Lara and myself), I was very keen to get the year 12 exam period over and done with.

These exams were an exclamation mark at the end of a long journey of formal education. Since she started at Primary School in 2007, she's been on countless excursions, incursions, camps and sports days. She's made speeches at Assembly and attended Anzac services. The same goes for High School. All of these activities had been hurtling her toward this moment. And, every one of those previous experiences has played an important part in bringing her to this point.

I recently heard someone talking about Chinese Bamboo. I don't know much about it myself. My parents had bamboo at their house and no-matter what we did, we never seemed to be able to stem its incredible growth. It was wild bamboo that seemed to make up its own rules. It didn't have a groovy name and this particular breed certainly wouldn't have been recommended as a sensible and effective screen by a landscape architect. I have since discovered that the growth of Chinese bamboo has some unique features. It requires fertile soil, watering, nurturing and sunshine. And then, for the first four years after its planting, there is no reward. There is nothing visible and no shoots above the ground. But, for these 4 years, the bamboo plant is putting its shoots way down deep. They are forming and growing and getting stronger. They are providing a foundation for a strong, healthy and beautiful plant. And then, in their fifth year, something remarkable happens. The bamboo shoots poke through the ground and then go on to grow 80 feet in six weeks.

The growth of the bamboo plant bears similarities to the education journey. Primary School is providing an incredible foundation for our children. All the activities, games, camps, excursions and learning experiences at school are laying the foundation for a strong future for our children. When you get up morning after morning, the routine can seem impossible. Washing lunchboxes, finding drink bottles, making sandwiches and desperately searching for the school hat. Tomorrow morning when this routine starts again, take a moment to see the incredible potential of your little person or people. Try to imagine for a moment what they will grow into and the difference that they are going to make in this world. It's a perspective changer.

Parenting is not the easiest task in the world. In fact, it's probably the most difficult thing that any of us could do. The task of nurturing, disciplining, guiding, mentoring and encouraging does not let up. Building character is a slow and laborious process. But it's laying the foundations for a solid future. So, keep on keeping on. Spend the time investing in your kids or grandkids and their future. Make sure that they are living in fertile soil. Nurture them, love them and prune them just enough to make sure that they grow and develop in the right direction. Take the time to thank their teachers and carers at school for the role that they are playing in their development as well. Most of all, enjoy this stage of life. It passes very quickly. And before you know it, you'll have your own 80-foot bamboo tree in the form of a teenage boy or girl. Do what you can to keep them pointing towards the sun. The book of Proverbs sums it up beautifully:

Proverbs 22 v 6: *Direct your children onto the right path, and when they are older, they will not leave it.*

POSSUM MAGIC

I recall a time when we decided to change from one major telecommunications carrier to another. A very "helpful" (if not a little clumsy) man came to our house to run some wires. He got on the roof, under the house and seemed to tramp around for hours. Approximately 2 weeks after he left there was a major downpour. Our roof started to leak and water came rushing down the wall in the lounge room. When a tile man came to inspect, he discovered that the clumsy cable man had removed two tiles and failed to put them back. The tile man put them in their rightful place and went on his way. Sadly, in the intervening period a possum had taken up residence in the roof. The possum was now trapped.

Over the course of the next 4-5 days, we tried to coax him out (to no avail). Things came to a head at 1.15 am one morning when we heard a terrifying crash. Unsure of where it had come from, we scouted inside and out. After a few more disturbing "bumps in the night" we eventually found a massive brush tail possum sitting bemused in our shower recess. This thing was enormous and dreadfully cranky. He had that look that people get when they disembark from a high-powered ride at Seaworld or Six-Flags. This feisty possum had fallen through the vent above the shower. I think both myself and the possum were equally as shocked to see each other. Of course, it could have been worse. He could have saved his stage dive for the moment when an unsuspecting family member was washing their hair.

I'd never looked deeply into the eyes of a huge possum before. Let alone while stumbling around in my "night clothes." What to do? After a short stand-off, I grabbed a towel and threw it over the possum. It was pure stealth on my part. I eventually managed to get him out of the house. (Of course, it may have been a she-possum. I didn't have the time or the expertise to make an informed decision). As I charged through the family room madly juggling this possum in a towel, Lara quickly threw open the back door and we (the massive marsupial and I) charged into the darkness; This must have been a ridiculous sight. It was pure adrenaline as far as I was concerned. I felt strangely alive and in control. Of course, we both knew that I was moments away from losing this battle. If I didn't release it when I did, Lara would be rushing me for a tetanus shot.

So, what's the point? This was an unexpected interruption for us. Life is full of unexpected interruptions. Most of them are far more serious than a wayward possum. Delays, frustrations and set-backs, things that come from left field and seem to squash or at least delay our plans and goals. Since we are always going to encounter them, we need to develop strategies to deal with them. While there are no easy answers, the following ideas may help to get you started:

- *Seek the advice and opinion of those whom you respect. A fresh perspective and some lateral thinking may be just what the Doctor ordered*
- *Roll with the punches (as much as you can). Make a judgment call and back yourself. Don't worry if initially you don't hit the mark. You can always modify your course as time goes by*
- *Keep an open mind. Some problems have more than one workable solution – so don't feel as though you have to find the only right answer.*
- *Don't lose your cool. You will only end up doing or saying something that you will regret. Take a few deep breaths before making any big decisions*
- *Never give up. When your plans unravel (as they often do) see this as an opportunity to do things in a different way (try and think outside the square)*

The book of Matthew, records one of Jesus' most famous statements. It's a statement that provides universal comfort to old and young alike:

Matthew 11 v 28 - 30: *Then Jesus said, "Come to me, all of you who are weary and carry heavy burdens, and I will give you rest. Take my yoke upon you, Let me teach you, because I am humble and gentle at heart, and you will find rest for your souls. For my yoke is easy to bear, and the burden I give you is light."*

EUROPEAN VACATION

After finishing year 12 in 2019, my eldest daughter Hannah decided that she wanted a gap year. So, with great enthusiasm, she deferred her course of study and decided to head overseas for 2020. I took a gap year after year 12 (my gap year was way back in 1990) and it was one of the best things I ever did. It gave me a chance to work out what I liked and what I didn't. I had many different jobs over the course of the year. I pumped petrol, drove a taxi truck, dug ditches, stacked shelves, painted a ski lodge and clambered around under houses as an electrician's labourer. A gap year gives you the chance to do a bit of everything. I loved mine.

So, I talked up the virtues of a gap year to Hannah. She enrolled herself in a YWAM (Youth with a Mission) course that happened to be in Spain (of all places!) These courses are a great introduction to mission work and they provide an excellent chance to gain some "hands on" experience serving others. The course itself was in Madrid. So, on 8 March 2020, Hannah and I set off together for a grand European adventure. My brief was to travel with her to Spain and settle her in. I quite liked this assignment. Prior to this, neither of us had ever been to Europe. So, this was kind of a big deal for both of us. After our long-haul flight via Doha, we arrived in Madrid on the Monday afternoon and immediately began exploring. Madrid is a wonderful city and there was so much to see. We had a ball.

Among other things, we ate crusty bread, we cycled the cobblestone streets; we poked around in markets; we saw a castle or two; we ate tapas in a bustling marketplace and we generally just embraced the beautiful ambiance of this historic city and its surroundings. A lazy walk around Avila was also a highlight. On the Thursday morning (3 days after our arrival) we were preparing to check out the base where Hannah would be staying for the following 5 months. As we were getting our bags ready to head out for the day, a message came through to Hannah's phone. The course had been cancelled! Wow! We didn't see this coming and it was a shock for both of us. Covid-19 had been steadily growing over the course of the week. It had made its way from Italy to Spain at breakneck speed. Hurried calls were made to our wonderful travel agent Liza and within 24 hours we were on a plane heading back to Melbourne.

It was a lot of travel for just 3.5 days. But nonetheless we had an epic time. It was awesome just being together. Just Dad and daughter. We had so much fun and we got so much achieved. I wouldn't swap it for anything.

I'm very conscious that Covid-19 changed everyone's version of reality. Social media, the press and the 6.00 pm news became saturated with nothing but Covid news. The news was usually quite grim and often overwhelming. It was a tough time for everyone. Melbourne spent 262 days in lockdown, which was the longest of any city in the world. But amongst the confusion and anxiety of the pandemic, there were also some golden opportunities. While the media inevitably ran stories about fights at the supermarket or panic buying and hoarding, never before have I seen so many opportunities for kindness and generosity. Despite the isolation that came from the lengthy lock-downs, I witnessed firsthand the kindness and generosity of neighbours, communities and complete strangers.

In difficult times, we all have a choice to make. Either we embrace the fear and become overwhelmed by the uncertainty or we make the decision to flex the kindness muscle. This will look different for every household and every individual. But I guarantee that most people saw more acts of generosity over the course of the pandemic than they had for years. Adversity gives each of us an excuse to show compassion, empathy, generosity and kindness. It actually provides the permission to serve others whom you wouldn't normally support. This phenomenon of care was a global response to Covid-19.

Whether it's your response to a global pandemic, or simply an opportunity to connect with the less fortunate, the pandemic helped us to modify our gaze. It gave all of us a chance to look beyond our own circumstances. It has enabled us to make some permanent changes and to keep looking out for mates, neighbours and strangers. For the first time ever, I witnessed on a grand scale the phenomenon of people treating others as they would like to be treated while they drew strength and comfort from those around them. While the uncertainty of Covid was very unsettling, it gave us a crash course in what it looks like to make the communities in which we live, happy, inclusive and interdependent. In the book of Matthew in the New Testament, we are given a nice little overview of the importance of serving others. The following passage demonstrates how profound our simple acts of kindness really can be.

Matthew 25 v 34-40: *Then the King will say to those on his right, "Come, you who are blessed by my Father, inherit the Kingdom prepared for you from the creation of the world. For I was hungry, and you fed me. I was thirsty, and you gave me a drink. I was a stranger, and you invited me into your home. I was naked, and you gave me clothing. I was sick, and you cared for me. I was in prison, and you visited me." Then these righteous ones will reply, "Lord when did we ever see you hungry and feed you? Or thirsty and give you something to drink? Or naked and give you clothing? When did we ever see you sick or in prison and visit you?" And the King will say, "I tell you the truth, when you did it to one of the least of these my brothers and sisters, you were doing it to me!"*

Little acts of kindness done for strangers are actually done for the Kingdom of Heaven and for the glory of God. It's a bit radical really. Keep looking for opportunities to flex the kindness muscle and I'll do the same.

NOMADIC DREAMING

Many years ago, in the pre-kids era, Lara and I decided to take a trip. We were renting a little unit in Box Hill North in the eastern suburbs of Melbourne. It was the first place that we lived after we got married. It was close to everything and it suited us perfectly. We had no pets and no debt. I had just finished my apprenticeship as a lawyer and I had roughly 6 months up my sleeve before I commenced my training to become a Barrister. Lara had a great job as an early childhood teacher at Carey Grammar in Kew.

We had NOT been contemplating a hippy adventure. But it suddenly dawned on us that we may not get clear air like this again until we were old and grey. So, we threw caution to the wind and decided to set-off to circumnavigate Australia. The first task was to find a suitable ride. We settled on a classic, light yellow 1975 VW Kombi. It was a pop-top camper with a fold out bed and a camp stove. It even had a fridge and a sink. While we had heard many horror stories about the unreliability of Kombis, we decided that a classic Kombi was an essential ingredient for a road trip such as this.

With very little in the way of concrete plans, we set off from Melbourne on a drizzly Sunday morning. It was March 1999. Our teary parents and an assortment of siblings gathered on the front lawn as we did our final checks before motoring slowly off down the street. Despite the grand adventure that lay before us, I drove off with a heavy heart as our families waved us away. Over the course of the next 5-6 months, we drove around the coast of Australia. We did a lot of free camping and we saw some incredible sights. We also met a swag of fascinating people.

As with most grand adventures, the people we met were as much a highlight as the places we went. We both fondly remember an elderly couple whom we met in Derby, in the far north of Western Australia. We had been free camping for a number of days on the Gibb River Road. This was about as remote a place as we could possibly be. On our way south, we decided to stop at the local Baptist Church. I somehow found myself delivering the Bible reading for the day and also bringing a greeting on behalf of Victorians generally. I got the impression that visitors were a bit of a novelty in these parts.

Following the service, we found ourselves having lunch with the Minister and his lovely wife back at their little home. They stretched the food and made us feel incredibly welcome. We discovered that people in remote corners of the country usually had the gift of hospitality. After lunch, I was directed to the lounge room and seated near the air conditioner. The day was sweltering. The elderly minister asked me whether I thought it was better to give than to receive. I felt it was a loaded question, but I agreed anyway. He told me to relax in the cool of their lovely little lounge room. He then disappeared. I knew not where.

When it came time to leave, we walked out to find our Kombi sparkling from top to bottom. This lovely elderly man, in searing heat, had washed 3 ½ months of mud and red dust from our van. I was overwhelmed. We had been feeling very isolated and a little homesick (Derby is a long way from Melbourne). In this simple yet profound act of service, both Lara and I somehow felt refreshed. It was more than a simple sponge and water. It was a symbol of utter service and sacrifice and generosity. I imagined that it was a bit like the way the disciples felt after Jesus had washed their feet. This story is found in John chapter 13.

John 13 v 4-9: *So he got up from the table, took off his robe, wrapped a towel around his waist, and poured water into a basin. Then he began to wash his disciples' feet, drying them with the towel he had around him. When Jesus came to Simon Peter, Peter said to him, "Lord, are you going to wash my feet?" Jesus replied, "You don't understand now what I am doing, but someday you will." "No," Peter protested, "you will never ever wash my feet!" Jesus replied, "Unless I wash you, you won't belong to me." Simon Peter exclaimed, "Then wash my hands and head as well. Lord, not just my feet!"*

John 14 v 12-17: *After washing their feet, he put on his robe again and sat down and asked, "Do you understand what I was doing? You call me 'Teacher' and 'Lord,' and you are right, because that's what I am. And since I, your Lord and Teacher, have washed your feet, you ought to wash each other's feet. I have given you an example to follow. Do as I have done to you. I tell you the truth, slaves are not greater than their master. Nor is the messenger more important than the one who sends the message. Now that you know these things, God will bless you for doing them."*

We can all name people that are so good at doing little acts of service. The fantastic thing is that we are all capable of such acts. Not only are we capable, but we're called. It is usually the little things that we do that can make a huge difference in the lives of others. It's important to be on the look-out for simple things you can do to brighten the lives of those around you. Mow a nature strip for someone who cannot. Bake a cake for someone who is feeling sad. Write a letter or a card to someone who is feeling lonely. Whatever you choose, enjoy the feeling of bringing joy, relief, satisfaction or comfort to someone who needs a boost.

And, by the way, the mighty Kombi was magnificent. We had it serviced in Cairns, Darwin and Fremantle. In 25,000 gruelling kilometres many of them on corrugated back roads, she just kept going. We crossed rivers, ate fresh crayfish, scuba dived on the Great Barrier Reef and lazed in pristine thermal springs in the Kimberly. It was the best foundation for our young marriage. If you see an opening (even just a little one) to squeeze in a nomadic adventure of your own, it comes highly recommended.

OLD BECOMES NEW

When I was a kid, I dreamed of one day owning a minibike. We had some rich friends who had minibikes in all shapes, sizes and colours. Occasionally we scammed a ride or two out of them. Sadly, these were few and far between. When I was 12, our family was on holiday in South Australia. We were stopped for petrol at a tiny little country service station when I spied a bright yellow Yamaha 80 for sale in the workshop. To cut a long story short, I talked Dad into letting me buy it. We managed to jam it into our people mover (only just) for a very cramped 8-hour drive back to Melbourne. We even pulled over in a truck-stop on the way home and took it for a fang. Even Mum had a ride. It's the only time I've ever seen my Mum ride a YZ 80. It gave me a lot of fun all those years ago. After many years of faithful service, it was getting old and rattly. I pulled it to bits in the early 1990's and stuck it in the shed. There it sat for almost 20 years. A number of years ago, I handed all the bits I could find over to my friendly motorcycle mechanic. It was to be a project for his spare time.

And what a project it became. After 12 months or so, he called me and told me that it was ready. Like an expectant father I nervously went to meet my new baby. It was beautiful. It turns out my mechanic is somewhat more meticulous than I am. Not only had it been rebuilt from top to bottom but considerable time and effort had been lashed on the finer details. My bike mechanic, Tim described this as the "bling." I took it for a couple of laps of the paddock and then safely bedded it down. My little bike that was once old, tired and broken now had a new lease of life. What was old had become new again.

I like the concept of old becoming new again, of things being restored or rejuvenated. Even better, I love the idea of people being restored or rejuvenated. It is very easy to let the responsibilities and pressures of our lives actually get the better of us. Without even realising it, the joy that should be ours somehow slips away. Despite being surrounded by stuff that is designed to make us happy, we end up feeling anything but. If you feel like this, then something has to change. Where to start? I'm not the happiness guru. Like everyone, I let the joy slip away from time to time. My observation, however, is that restoration or rejuvenation often come when we manage to look beyond our immediate circumstances. That is, if we are able to adopt a worldview that doesn't see the universe revolving around ourselves, then this is probably a positive start. I have a close friend who talks about the fact that we all have a "me switch." Many of us cruise through life with our "me switch" turned firmly on. One of the challenges is to work out how to switch it off. While this will look different for everyone, it's an absolute necessity if we're going to live in a fulfilling, engaged and purposeful way.

An active interest in the well-being of others, a sense of community spirit and participation in some kind of service are all things that can help to foster a new outlook. Not only can these things provide a sense of involvement and connection, but they often breed feelings of fulfilment and accomplishment.

Furthermore, I would not have been a School Chaplain for 13 years if I didn't think that restoration and rejuvenation can also be tied to a sense of spiritual well-being or spiritual fulfilment. Obviously, this will mean different things to different people. Read a book, talk to a friend, knock on a door or two. There are plenty of ways to find out more about this kind of stuff. Analyse yourself from time to time just to see how you're travelling. We can't be happy and fulfilled all the time. But if you are feeling old, tired and overwhelmed, don't panic. I know exactly how you feel. I've been there too. Reach out, connect and breathe. Don't be afraid to let people into your world. This may be a slow and tortuous process and you may need plenty of help to get there. Friends, doctors, pastors, teachers, parents, siblings, a local faith community and neighbours may all play a role. Think about the resources around you and put your hand up for help.

Psalm 121 v 1-8: *I look up to the mountains – does my help come from there? My help comes from the Lord who made heaven and earth! He will not let you stumble; the one who watches over you will not slumber. Indeed, he who watches over Israel never slumbers or sleeps. The Lord himself watches over you! The Lord stands beside you as your protective shade. The sun will not harm you by day, nor the moon at night. The Lord keeps you from all harm and watches over your life. The Lord keeps watch over you as you come and go, both now and forever.*

By the way, did riding my "brand new" 34-year-old Yamaha 80 put a smile on my face? You betcha!

The lads outside my childhood home – I'm on the left. Next to me is my older brother Andrew, then my younger brother Luke. My young cousin Cam is on the other scooter with my best mate from primary school Jonny. Jonny and I remain best mates having met in grade 5 at Blackburn Lake Primary school in 1982

Lara and I heading off to her university valedictory dinner in 1991. The car is an XB Fairmont that I bought in 1990 for $1500. I wish I kept it! Lara kept her dress. Unlike my XB, Lara's dress is not as fashionable as it once was.

Myself and brother Andrew in full legal regalia having just moved the admission of our younger brother Luke as a Lawyer of the Supreme Court of Victoria (1999). Lara and I flew home from Darwin for the ceremony. A proud day for Mum, Dad and our Uncle Murray (also a lawyer)

This was our beloved 1975 Kombi that we bought in 1998 for our lap of Australia. This photo was taken just before we set off down the Gibb River Road in the Kimberly region of WA. We were away for over 5 months on this grand adventure. We did nearly 25,000 km's and the Kombi was simply amazing.

Classic Christmas Day shot (2014) at my Granny's house. Each year, we would gather for morning tea at Granny's house. It was a great time to be together as an extended family before heading in different directions – Christmas has always been a big deal in our family.

Pre-Christmas celebrations with Lara's family at our home in 2018. We do this every year and it is always great fun. With so many cousins, we opt for a pre-Christmas gathering so we can catch up with family that we don't get to see on Christmas Day. I inherited a wonderful family when I married Lara.

My Gracie on the mobility scooter while my Granny (aka GG) looks on. Gracie
and William had way more fun on this thing than GG.

Our first ever family Mission trip to The Philippines in 2015. Here we are with our close friend and mentor Pastor Choi in Ligao City. Pastor Choi and his family (his wife Alma and their son Biggs) are our Filipino family – They are very precious people and supremely committed to serving Jesus in everything they do.

Killing time before boarding a plane from LAX to Melbourne in 2016. The In-N-Out Burger is perched directly below the flight path. It's a great place to eat a burger or two before the long flight home.

One of our coastal adventures in our beloved Bedford bus (in the background). The old school bus (affectionately named Bustin-Loose) is a great way to travel and has created lots of family memories. This photo was taken on the NSW coast.

This was Gracie's first day at Carey Grammar in 2020. Carey has been an important part of our family tradition. My Grandpa (Brian Baird) and my Dad both attended Carey as kids, as did all my uncles. Grandpa and Dad also taught there. Myself and my brothers all attended Carey as did our kids.

This photo was taken in March 2020 in a laneway in Madrid, Spain. I accompanied Hannah on the first leg of her YWAM gap year adventure. Hannah and I had a wonderful couple of days touring Madrid together before the world began shutting down due to Covid-19. After only 4 nights in Spain, we packed our bags and flew back to Melbourne before the borders were slammed shut.

Myself and the beloved Marianne (aka Mez). I got to know Mez in 2008 when I started my Chaplaincy at Blackburn Primary School. Back then she was a grade 1 teacher. As at the writing of this book she is now the Assistant Principal. She has been a wonderful friend to our family over many years and we love spending time with her. She has always been a great supporter of the Chaplaincy program and of me personally.

Here are the amazing Principals of Blackburn Primary that I worked with during my time as the school Chaplain. Andrew Cock on my left, with Clayton Sturzaker and Sue Barclay (nee Henderson) on my right. This photo was taken at my farewell breakfast in December 2020.

This was the morning of Lara's 50th birthday. Her sister Nessa is on the right with Nessa's amazing husband Cam in the middle. To celebrate Lara's birthday, we spent a few days with them at their home in Ocean Grove.

For my 50th Birthday, we rented a house in Paynesville on the Gippsland Lakes –
On the day of my actual birthday we hired a little boat and cruised with the family
around the waterways. The highlight was lunch on the Banksia Peninsula. I first
visited the Banksia Peninsula on my Year 7 school camp.

Me and my boys at Wattle Park Golf Course in February 2023. As Charlie and William get better, my game seems to get worse. Nonetheless, golfing for me is a social exercise and I love the chance to get out with the boys for a round or two.

This is one of my favourite photos – This was taken in January 2022 on a windswept day at Carpenter Rocks SA. Following our annual summer Beach Mission in Portland, we joined Mum and Dad at their Beach House at nearby Blackfellows Caves. It was their happy space and a place of supreme rest and retreat.

This was taken in August 2023 to commemorate the 100-year celebrations of Carey Grammar. We gathered as a family and had a tour of the school with the Simpson kids that were still current students. This was a special day and the first time we'd been together as brothers and families with Mum and Dad since before Covid.

SUPER COACH

For many years now I have fantasised about getting a water craft of some description. Ideally, it would be a gnarly and very sleek custom ski boat with all the gadgets in the world. I frequently suggest joint venture type arrangements to my family members. The best-case scenario would be to go halves with someone who is allergic to sun, water and sand. If I ever found a financial partner with this rare phobia, I would be sure to give them frequent updates as to how their share of the vessel was performing. Even better, if they happened to be a member of a support group for those who are allergic to sun, water and sand, I'd make some diplomatic enquiries as to whether any of their mates wanted to branch out and go halves in a jet-ski.

I've come close to buying a speedboat a couple of times, but I've never been game enough to take the plunge. Lara once called my bluff on this. After weeks of dreaming and discussion, she said, "just do it – go and get one." Talk about reverse psychology. I'm not sure what books she'd been reading or where she did her PhD in psychology, but it suddenly gave me terrible cold feet. Once I knew that I had the green light to buy a boat, I started thinking about all the reasons why I probably didn't need my own boat. I still don't have one.

I think that I was very attracted to the concept because a boat for me symbolises leisure. While I'll continue to talk about such a purchase, it's very unlikely to happen. I'm ok with that and I'll continue to scour eBay and marketplace for bargains. That will probably have to suffice. A number of years ago, I took my kids up to Victoria's beautiful Lake Eildon for a Dad and kids water ski weekend. The sun was shining and the boats were out in force. There were all manner of ski boats coming and going. Most had unique names plastered along the side. Some are not suitable for this timeslot! It was a rich cultural experience to say the least. There were sunburnt yobbos as far as the eye could see with all manner of floatation devices including oversized blow-up swans and flamingos. We had a ball.

I rode in a boat or two and watched a number of new hopefuls try their luck on the wakeboard. It's like a snowboard but for the water. There was no end of advice being dispensed from those inside the boat. "Lie back, bend your knees, keep your board pointing forward, don't stand up too quickly." I must say that after an hour or so sitting in the boat and watching all this unfold, I became a bit of an expert myself. I, too, found myself identifying why people were failing to stand up and keep their balance.

The difficulty of course in me dispensing advice as a would-be wakeboard instructor was that I had never wake boarded myself and I had absolutely no idea how to do it. But I felt that all my observations had placed me in a unique position to provide helpful feedback. On my previous water ski attempt (circa 1990), I was hardly a Moomba Master. In short, I was the last person you'd turn to for technical tips when it comes to wake boarding or anything related to boating for that matter.

As I reflect on all of this, I realise that there is a big difference between dispensing advice and offering encouragement. I was actually in no position to dispense advice. But I was certainly in a position to cheer on the budding wake boarders from the boat. Despite having no clue about technique, I could still share in the joy of their success when they got it right. I think that this is an important lesson for life. I'm sure that we all know people who are talkers rather than listeners. Those people who are quick to offer their advice on every aspect of our lives. The danger is that their advice is often couched in the language of judgement, disapproval or criticism. Furthermore, I frequently find that these people don't have the credentials to be offering the advice that they so willingly give. Sound familiar?

All of us have the tendency to want to advise others, particularly when we believe that we can solve what we perceive to be their problems. However, in nearly every one of these cases, we would be of much greater value to our friend, family or neighbour if we listened, reflected and encouraged. An exceedingly practical piece of advice is found in the New Testament book of Ephesians, 4 v 29 where it says: *Do not let any unwholesome talk come out of your mouths, but only what is helpful for building others up according to their needs, that it may benefit those who listen.* NIV

It's good advice. Why don't you see if it works for you? BTW, late in the day (and on my 5th attempt) I did manage to burst forth from the water with the wake board attached. It was a sight to behold and a memory I'll treasure! I'm sure that with a dozen or so trips to the osteopath, I'll be able to do it again someday.

WRONG PASSCODE - TRY AGAIN

I recall a moment in time before everyone in the world had mobile phones or the internet. Life seemed much less complicated. When you went home from work on Friday night, nobody got the chance to aggravate you until Monday morning. These days we are so wired that we barely get a chance to switch off.

Before the iPhone, my kids had iPods. Does anyone still use them? I recall the joy my kids got from mucking around on them. They took photos, listened to music and played games. The iPod was really the first experience the kids had to set up their own pass code. We encouraged this and we talked about how important it was not to share their code with friends or siblings. Somewhere along the line, my boy Charlie decided to change his pass code. This was in response to a catastrophic breach by his younger brother William who had cracked his code. The problem was, that after changing his pass code, he promptly forgot what it was (sadly, I think he inherited this affliction from his father).

He tried without success to punch in as many codes as he possibly could. He punched in all manner of combinations that he thought he may have used. He believes that he got close to the actual code. Not close enough as it turns out. By the time he had finished his frenzied guessing game, he was well and truly shut out. In fact, his iPod was DISABLED for 22,398,802 minutes. Yes, that's a long time. It's 15,553 days or 42.6 years to be precise. I pictured him finally turning his iPod back on in 2055 at the age of 52 (this pass-code disaster took place in 2013). By this time, Lara and myself would be well into our 80's. With any luck the family would all gather at our nursing home to watch Charlie's iPod come back on-line. I suspect by then that his own grandchildren would be bickering about who was going to get the first go. Lara and I would probably get overwhelmed by the commotion and need to have a tablet and a rest.

It did make me think about what everyone will be doing in 42.6 years from now. How old will you be in 42.6 years? Inevitably, many of our loved ones will have passed on. After all, it's a very long way off. Our school kids will be established in their careers, have sprawling families of their own and will be working out how on earth to spend our money. When you start thinking like this, it can be a bit overwhelming. For me, it had the effect of making me think about how precious life really is. Time will march on. Things won't stay the same. It made me perform my own little stock-take. I started asking myself whether there were things I could be doing better. The answer is YES. Are there things that I am taking for granted? The answer to that is also YES. Am I spending time and energy on things that will ultimately amount to very little? YES again. I must state for the record, that this has been a positive exercise. While there is definitely room for improvement, I have managed to identify a few things that I wouldn't change. That's a bonus.

We often talk about how things in our lives would change if we discovered that we had a short time to live. What would you do if you knew you only had 42 days to live? Would your attitude be different if you knew you had at least another 42.6 years? For me, regardless of what lies ahead, it's important to live with a sense of purpose and direction. Whether it's 42 days or 42 years, the greatest rewards come when you live intentionally.

Regardless of what the future holds, it's inevitable that your actions, attitudes and outlook will have a profound effect on your life and the lives of your children and even your future grandchildren. Decisions made in the here and now can set the scene for generations to come. Take some time to stop and think about what kind of family you want to have in 42.6 years. Regardless of whether you're around to see it, start setting the tone for what will follow.

Take nothing for granted, act on your dreams and start making the changes that you know you need to make. Spend less time worrying about stuff that doesn't matter and more time thinking about the stuff that does.

Psalm 39 v 4 – 7 says: *Lord, remind me how brief my time on earth will be. Remind me that the days are numbered–how fleeting my life is. You have made my life no longer than the width of my hand. My entire life is just a moment to you; at best, each of us is but a breath. We are merely shadows, and all our busy rushing ends in nothing. We heap up wealth, not knowing who will spend it. And so, Lord, where do I put my hope? My only hope is in you.*

POOR TRIXIE

M y family frequently travels to Portland, Victoria for the school holidays. It's a big drive from Melbourne, almost as far as the South Australian border. We've been going to Portland for many years and have spent every summer holiday there since 1980. We started going there as part of a Scripture Union summer kids' program and we just never stopped. It is, therefore, a place that has lots of memories for me and my whole family. Not only do Lara and my kids love it, but over the years both my brothers (Andrew and Luke) were also very involved in the holiday program. You could say that it's in our DNA. Mum and Dad are still involved. They loved the people of Portland so much that they pulled up their deep roots in suburban Melbourne and moved there to pastor the Baptist Church.

I recall one New Year's Eve (circa 1995). I drove out to visit a farming family that I knew to pick up some hay bales for a New Year's Eve bush dance. I was driving an old V8 Fairlane and I had a tandem trailer strapped on behind. A V8 Fairlane coupled to a tandem trailer is a very masculine combination. I felt pretty cool as I cruised out to my friend's farm, all footloose and fancy free, a powerful car and an open road. With the help of a mate, we loaded the hay bales up and set off for town. As I was driving off, I felt the most minor bump somewhere up the back of the trailer. I thought I should stop and just make sure that everything was OK. Sadly, the minor bump was the resident Jack Russell Terrier (and a beloved pet) being clipped by my tandem trailer. OH DEAR!

This was new territory for me. I am an animal lover at heart and the thought of inflicting injury, pain, death on anything at all was almost too much to bear. But running over someone else's pet has an additional layer of complexity. This is particularly so when the 20-year-old owner of the said pet is the second person on the scene. Nobody knew where to look. I didn't know the dog well enough to burst into tears. Obviously the same couldn't be said for the owner (who later declared that he got the dog for his fifth birthday!) I and the owner eventually exchanged a very clumsy embrace.

There were a few tears before poor old Trixie was bundled into the car for a mercy dash to town. Sadly, for me and the owner (and Trixie of course), she didn't get to enjoy too much of 1996 (a few hours from memory). I think she just managed to see in the New Year before going to Doggy Heaven. Some of you will no doubt have been in a similar situation. There are no rules for unchartered territory like this. I realised, however, that in this situation, it was helpful to try and strike the balance between remorse, empathy and shame. It's not always easy!

While most of you probably haven't run over someone else's prized pet, I'm sure you've all been in situations where you have been stumped about how to act or react. Sometimes it is very difficult to know what to do. Sometimes things just sneak up on you and you feel flawed by them. Maybe you've been blindsided by the loss of a job, the loss of a friendship, a serious illness or the death of someone significant. Sometimes we're just left asking WHY? Can I suggest that it is ok to be stumped by these kinds of events? We're not designed to just take them in our stride. We can't possibly have answers for everything or solutions for every problem. We're all far too human for that.

So, next time something stops you in your tracks, don't be too hard on yourself. Give yourself permission to flounder before you start picking up the pieces. As for my sad and awkward predicament, grace reigned supreme. The beautiful family that owned Trixie were very forgiving and gracious. They didn't blame me or treat me any differently. They didn't lose their cool or say things that they later needed to apologise for. I love the advice from the Apostle Paul in the book of Ephesians.

Ephesians 4 v 31-32: *Get rid of all bitterness, rage, anger, harsh words, and slander, as well as all types of evil behaviour. Instead, be kind to each other, tender-hearted, forgiving one another, just as God through Christ has forgiven you.*

My dear and gracious friends displayed genuine kindness and empathy even in the midst of their own pain. Their response and attitude was 100% genuine and amazing and taught me some important life lessons and for that I'm extremely grateful.

KEW TRAFFIC SCHOOL

Ever since I was a little boy, I looked very longingly every time we drove past the Kew Traffic School. It's a mini village with mini shops, parks, roads, traffic lights and pedestrian crossings. We would sometimes see other kids riding their bikes around this little village and wonder why we never got to. Sadly, I never managed to get there as a child despite my great desire to do so. A great bonus of having kids of your own is that you sometimes get to do stuff that you missed when you were a kid. Over the course of our time at our local kindergarten, each of my kids got to go on an excursion to the Kew Traffic School. It has always been one of my favourite excursions and I was keen to volunteer to be a parent helper on this one.

In gearing up for Traffic School, I was reminded that I was yet to teach my 5-year-old Gracie how to ride her bike without training wheels. My little Gracie rightly pointed out that I hadn't given her enough "training." That was all I needed. With just over an hour to go before the bus departed with children and bikes on board, I whipped out a spanner and took off Gracie's training wheels. It was a drastic and hurried response to my feelings of failure for not having taught my daughter to ride unassisted. I pushed her up and back a few times through the local park. This was far from a straightforward exercise. I then looked for the highest point in the park (which is over by the pine tree) and then decided that this was a good spot to launch her down the hill. After a few practice runs I determined that she was ready.

Riding a bike is second nature to most of us. If you know how to ride a bike you don't actually have to think about how to balance. You don't turn your mind to the mechanics of it. Rather, you just jump on and ride. This can make the process of teaching someone else a little frustrating. While I just wanted to push Gracie down the (very) little hill, my 5-year-old wanted me to hold tightly onto the bars while I pushed her around. In actual fact this made the process a whole lot harder. Gracie found herself fighting against me and we were both pulling the handlebars in opposite directions. It didn't exactly bolster her confidence and I almost slipped a disc in the process. I ended up sweaty and puffed and aching. Despite being terrified about letting go, I eventually bit the bullet and with a push she was off and going. She rode all by herself. Not once, but a number of times. What a great Dad moment.

I suspect that we all find ourselves faced with tasks and challenges that we simply don't feel we can cope with. Maybe we feel this way because we lack confidence. Perhaps fear keeps us from attempting things that we may actually be quite good at. Do you ever find yourself passing up opportunities simply because you don't know where to start or what to do? If you can ride a bike, chances are that at some point in time your dad, mum, brother, sister or grandparent simply let go of you and left you to your own devices. You probably fell off. That's part of it. But you eventually got the hang of it. You'd never be able to ride if you didn't take a risk, have the occasional stack, skin your knees and get back up and keep moving forward. In this respect, learning to ride a bike is a great metaphor for life. In life you will only improve, gain confidence and deal with your inadequacies and fears if you are committed to actually having a go. This occasionally involves straying outside your comfort zone. It's important to remember that challenges and trials are OK. Don't panic when this happens. All is not lost! In his letter to the Romans, the Apostle Paul makes a classic and profound observation:

Romans 5 v 3-6: *We can rejoice, too, when we run into problems and trials, for we know that they help us develop endurance. And endurance develops strength of character, and character strengthens our confident hope of salvation. And this hope will not lead to disappointment. For we know how dearly God loves us, because he has given us the Holy Spirit to fill our hearts with his love. When we were utterly helpless, Christ came at just the right time and died for us sinners.*

We had a great day at the traffic school as anticipated. Gracie was so chuffed at being able to ride without training wheels. Despite the hard work in getting her riding on her own, it all paid off in the end. It was a proud moment for both dad and daughter.

WILL I EVER LEARN?

I occasionally find myself in the Melbourne CBD for work. When I walk from the car-park to my Chambers, I walk past the Melbourne Magistrates' Court. This sits on the corner of William and Lonsdale Streets. In my job, I predominantly appear for people who have been charged by the Police for criminal offending. Most of my work is conducted in the Magistrates' Court. While there are Courthouses dotted all over the suburbs and regional Victoria, I spend a fair bit of time at the Melbourne Court. The steps of the Melbourne Magistrates' Court are always an interesting place. If you're a people watcher, then this little corner of the world is about as interesting as things get. There are always comings and goings. Not only are there defendants coming and going, but they are often joined by their extended families. Some are happy, some sad, some stressed. All are desperately hoping that their loved one leaves via the same door that they entered the Court complex. Nobody wants to go out the naughty door. The naughty door ensures a bumpy ride in a white prison van. That's the least palatable way to leave a Courthouse.

The steps of the Court are a little microcosm. Those standing on the steps usually fit quite neatly into three categories and can often be readily identified by their clothes and accessories. If you're holding a briefcase, you're a member of the legal profession. If you're holding a big diary, you're a detective. If you're pushing a pram, you're usually a defendant or a doting partner. That's just the way things are.

Anyway, on this particular occasion, I spied a young man sitting on the steps. What caught my attention was the slogan on his T-shirt. It simply read (in very large letters) "Will I ever learn?" I chuckled and thought to myself that this is the last shirt I would choose to wear on the morning of my court case. It closely rivals the T-shirt worn by a defendant at the Ballarat Court. His T-shirt was emblazoned with the slogan "Drive it like you stole it." Again, a poor choice for Court. I hope he hadn't been charged with stealing a car.

As we look back over our lives, we will all be able to identify some highlights and lowlights. Most of us won't have too much trouble identifying times when we made mistakes or did the wrong thing. It happens to all of us. Poor choices, bad decisions or monumental mistakes are things that we can all identify with. Hopefully, however, the older we get the less we fall victim to these happenings. The theory is that each time we muck things up, we actually learn from our shortfalls and try to do better next time. The real tragedy exists when things never seem to change. We all know people who make the same mistake over and over again. Perhaps you're that person. It's frustrating to watch and it's debilitating to live with. Despite the pain of poor choices, for some people, things never seem to get any better.

In a family situation, poor choices are a fairly common occurrence (they are in my family anyway). I've seen a few and I'm sure we'll see plenty more. The challenge is to deal with these in a constructive way. While the overwhelming temptation is to blow your stack when things go bad, it's important to look instead for an opportunity to turn the lowlight into a teaching moment. When I reflect on my own childhood and teenage years, my parents did a remarkable job to balance appropriate discipline with golden teaching moments. Rather than exploding, they worked hard to help us to connect actions with consequences. We always knew when Mum and Dad were displeased, but they never flexed their muscles just for the sake of it. Being from a family of three boys (relatively close in age) there were plenty of challenges for my dear parents. We gave them many opportunities to exercise grace, patience and forgiveness.

At some stage, we all had earthly parents. Some of them did a great job at being the parents that we needed them to be. However, some parents don't have the first clue about raising kids. Instead of having a memory bank full of good memories, for some of us, our parents created nothing but sadness and trauma. It's an all too familiar story. If this is your experience, it's essential that you know that you have a Heavenly Father who loves you way more than your earthly father ever does or did. Psalm 103 (5) talks about a God who *"fills my life with good things. My youth is renewed like the eagle's."*

Psalm 103 v 6-13 also provides some wonderful words of encouragement:

The Lord gives righteousness and justice to all who are treated unfairly. He revealed his character to Moses and his deeds to the people of Israel. The Lord is compassionate and merciful, slow to get angry and filled with unfailing love. He will not constantly accuse us, nor remain angry forever. He does not punish us for all our sins; he does not deal harshly with us, as we deserve. For his unfailing love toward those who fear him is as great as the height of the heavens above the earth. He has removed our sins as far from us as the east is from the west. The Lord is like a father to his children, tender and compassionate to those who fear him.

Our Heavenly Father gives us plenty of second chances and plenty of opportunities to learn and grow. Work with Him on this stuff and let Him transform you into the person that you were born to be.

RUNAWAY MOWER

Garden maintenance is not particularly high on my list of priorities. I love the look of a beautiful garden. I just don't consistently set aside time to do what's required to have a beautiful garden. I do have moments of inspiration, but these are few and far between. I recall one afternoon while I was dutifully mowing my lawn when a car pulled up in my street. The visitor was a lovely lady who turns up occasionally at the invitation of Lara to demonstrate skin-care products. It's like an expensive game of show and tell. After 20 or so minutes we buy stuff, everyone is happy and she gets on her way. She's delightful and I'm pretty sure she'd still pop over even if we didn't buy a thing.

When I saw her arrive, I shut down the mower and we had a brief chat. I began to brace myself for an expensive afternoon. Just as I was commenting on her funky shoes, I heard a strange noise. I turned and (to my horror) I saw that the mower had begun to roll down the footpath. It had gathered a fair bit of pace too. I dashed out the gate just in time to see it leave the footpath and merge (somewhat unsafely) onto the road. I know that most people would regard me as "fast twitch." I'm quite obviously designed for pace (stop laughing). Sadly, however, not even my gazelle-like speed could reign in the out-of-control Masport. It was a handicap race and the mower's lead was simply punishing. All I could do was watch as the mower collided with force into the rear of the skin lady's shiny car. This would have been ok if the mower wasn't travelling backwards. It was the metal handle that hit the car's boot and tail light. It made a loud crunching noise.

This was an awkward moment. It could have been worse though. The skin lady instantly forgave my terrible blunder and her first words were, "Don't worry about the car." Very fortunately for me, there was no panel or lens damage. There was an exchange of paint which I managed to buff out while she was dispensing product to my skin-conscious family. By the end of my minor detailing job, the car looked spic and span and everyone was happy. This could have been a whole lot more embarrassing. While my level of grief would certainly have been far greater had there been a busted light or panel damage, I'm quite sure that the skin lady's response would have been exactly the same. In fact, her response seemed to have nothing at all to do with whether there was any damage or not. She instantly put me at ease and she didn't cast any blame in my direction, even though it was my fault.

It's fair to say that this wouldn't be the reaction of everyone. It's so hard sometimes to moderate our responses when unexpected things happen. Often, if stuff like this happens, our reaction can be one of anger, judgement or the blame game. There is a sense in which each of these emotions are understandable when something of yours is broken, scratched or otherwise damaged by the inattention or carelessness of someone else. We are all human. But the skin lady's response was gracious, forgiving and kind. I'm not sure whether she had trained herself to respond in this way or whether she's naturally very chilled and understanding. What I do know is that it's possible to take a deep breath when stuff like this happens and make a choice about our first response. It is possible to put relationships and people before stuff if we really put our mind to it.

In the same way that we've always needed grace and forgiveness in the past, we all need to do our best to extend grace and forgiveness to others going forward. Being parents (in particular) gives us all plenty of practice to develop these skills. So, next time your child scrapes something, drops something (a new iPhone for example) or makes another accidental blunder, do your best to respond the way the skin lady did.

It's a big challenge, but it will go a long way towards building love, trust and character into the ones that you love. None of this means that we live in a world without consequences. Consequences are a fact of life and sometimes we have to deal with them. I like the saying "What they see, is what they'll be." Teach your kids by your own example, the path of grace and forgiveness and, with any luck, they'll practice these important life skills for themselves.

I love the words in Ephesians Chapter 4 v 2-3:

Always be humble and gentle. Be patient with each other, ...making allowance for each other's faults because of your love. Make every effort to keep yourselves united in the Spirit, binding yourselves together with peace.

DRIVE-IN THEATRE

O n one particular summer holiday, our family participated in the great Australian tradition of seeing a movie at the Drive-in. I suspect that plenty of kids these days haven't had the chance to go to a Drive-in. They are not as accessible as they once were. Most Drive-in theatres have been sold and turned into housing developments, car parks or shopping centres. The first drive-in theatre in Australia was opened in February 1954 in Burwood, Victoria. I recall as a child (maybe grade 3 or 4) going to a double feature at the Burwood Drive-in with my family.

Going to a Drive-in with kids is difficult enough. I can now say this from personal experience. I can't imagine why my parents thought that a double feature would be a good idea. Even 40 years later, it stands out as a great memory though. I recall cramming into the car with pillows and blankets. From memory, we also took a mate. While we all did our best to see what was happening on the big screen, we were distracted by the play equipment. We pestered our parents for food and we spent most of the night running backwards and forwards to the toilets.

As I look back now, I wonder about the movie combination showing at our double feature. The first movie was "Nine to Five" starring Dolly Parton. Released in 1980, this movie was a classic. The second movie was "Chariots of Fire." This movie is based on true events surrounding the 1924 Olympic games. Eric Liddell (a devout Scottish Christian) runs in the games for the glory of God, while Harold Abrahams (an English Jew) runs to overcome prejudice. I still can't make the connection between these wonderful historical events and Dolly Parton. Maybe I'm overthinking it. Perhaps I need to step back a bit and squint. In any event, the movies didn't seem very compatible then and they don't seem any more compatible now. I can't imagine that those committed to a Dolly Parton movie would also think that Chariots of fire was a good night out. We did get a bit sleepy during the serious movie.

Decades later, when we took our own kids to the Drive-in, it was a sensible single movie at Dromana. My kids stretched out, the adults sat on deck chairs and all manner of sweet treats were consumed. It was a fantastic summer evening. I sometimes wonder whether my own kids will remember the time they went to the Muppet movie at the Dromana Drive-in with the same fondness that I recall my own childhood experience at Burwood. Will they remember it at all? I hope so. That is the fabulous thing about holidays. They are a chance to create experiences that will eventually turn into memories. While school holidays do provide ample opportunity to create family memories, it is also really important to look for opportunities to keep this going when the routine and humdrum of life sets in.

It's important to look for little opportunities to add to the family memory bank. This doesn't always involve spending buckets of money (or any money at all). It's a trap to equate disposable income or wealth with contentment or happiness. Money comes and goes and ultimately guarantees nothing when it comes to happiness or purpose. If you strive for contentment and the simple things in life, you may just stumble across a rare form of family bliss.

In 1 Timothy 6 v 6-8 we are reminded of a very important lesson:

Yet true godliness with contentment is itself great wealth. After all, we brought nothing with us when we came into the world, and we can't take anything with us when we leave it. So if we have enough food and clothing, let us be content.

Maybe take the kids on a train ride or catch the bus to the shopping centre. Load up the bikes and take a ride along your favourite creek or river. Take the kids for a non-essential walk around the shops. I don't mean the weekly shop – this has the potential for creating bad memories for parents and children alike! Or go and look at the big ships coming and going at your closest port. I saw a young mum recently perched on the pedestrian overpass near my house with a toddler or two watching the big yellow diggers as they broke ground on a new residential tower. The kids were engrossed. Who doesn't love a good digger? It doesn't matter what you do, if you're together and having fun, you're kicking goals.

LISTEN, WATCH, LEARN, ENCOURAGE AND LISTEN SOME MORE

Most of us probably think that we have a pretty good idea of what makes our child or children tick. Sometimes we can identify pretty early where the interest of a particular child lies. For those of us with multiple children, it's usually not too hard to identify which of our kids can kick a footy, catch a ball or shoot a hoop. Some kids can just do these things and often display these natural abilities from an early age. Kids who enjoy sport will usually play from dawn until dusk.

Equally, as parents we can all usually tell which of our children haven't quite grasped the idea of sport. Even though we can coax them outside for a game, these kids can often feel more at home drawing, reading, gaming or building stuff. None of this is to say that the two categories are mutually exclusive. They're not. But in my experience a child will usually show a natural inclination toward one area over another.

As parents it's great to be able to identify the interests of each child so that we can spend time nurturing these interests and play an active role in helping to build confidence into each of them. By now you'll be thinking about how you are going with your own children. I assure you that there is a fair bit of hit and miss associated with this process. And don't panic if you miss the mark here and there. Not only will young kids usually show an interest in everything, they also pick things up and put them down quickly while they're working this stuff out.

I have absolutely no interest in anything scientific. I never understood maths and I still get very nervous with anything involving numbers. In year 10, it was suggested that "Business Maths" might be more my thing. Similarly, I was advised against any form of mathematics in years 11 and 12. I foolishly decided to do year 11 accounting which

I failed despite many hours of expert tutoring from a family friend. You would think that the warning signs were flashing from a very young age, but apparently not. For years my parents persisted in giving me highly educational and scientific gifts for successive birthday and Christmas presents. From about the age of 9, I was given a Spirograph, a 50-in-1-electronics set, a chemistry set, a microscope and my very own calculator. Whenever anybody asked, my family would say that Phil is the scientific one. I have zero idea where they got this idea. Maybe they'd seen me kick a footy and just hoped that I'd be good at something. And while I didn't mind these presents, I was much happier when the skateboard finally arrived.

There are many challenges associated with being a parent. We have the job of provider, encourager and mentor. It is also our task to set boundaries and to provide the discipline our children need. In amongst this difficult balancing act, it is important that we take the time to really understand how our children work. Spend time bouncing around ideas about what they enjoy. Try new activities and go to new places. Help them to think outside the square. You'll probably end up spending an arvo or two at the footy when all they wanted was Scienceworks, the museum or the library. You might get them a soccer ball when all they wanted was a fishing rod. Don't panic about these little faux pas. They are all part of the process. The challenge is to get it mostly right most of the time. The important thing is to try. Listen, watch, learn, encourage and listen some more. If you do this, you can't go too far wrong.

As a parent, children are our greatest blessing. This doesn't mean that they always bring delight. They have the potential to produce the greatest challenges that we could ever imagine. But, it's important to remember that as we do our best to understand, nurture, bless, shepherd and love our kids, we must always try to do it from a position of peace and gratitude. No sense in winding our kids up or engaging in unnecessary conflict. Instruction, understanding and a peaceful attitude are the keys.

The Apostle Paul reminds us that one of the keys to life is to live in peace. I love it when I meet someone who is truly at peace. It doesn't matter what's going on around them, they seem to have a supernatural ability to remain unflappable. There is no question that this is a significant superpower when it comes to raising kids. I confess to having had some rather epic fails when it comes to this aspect of parenting. Despite this, I don't give up and I keep working on this stuff. In my experience, real and genuine sustained peace can only come from Christ. Paul writes about this in Colossians 3 v 15:

And let the peace that comes from Christ rule in your hearts. For as members of one body you are called to live in peace. And always be thankful.

ROAST NIGHT

In my home, Monday night is roast night. It's the night that none of the kids want to miss. We all just know that on Monday night we all gather for a Christmas style feast. It's a great time to be together and we love the chance to sit around the table. Even though life is busy and kids are working or at Uni, they all make the effort to be present on Mondays. Everyone is welcome and there are often a few additions to our table on roast night.

Family time is such a blessing and, in particular, time around the dining or kitchen table is so important. One of my own kids once remarked that they wished we all ate breakfast together like we used to do. I'd forgotten actually how uncomplicated things used to be when the kids were small. When all my kids were at primary school, we would often sit down and eat breaky together. It doesn't happen much these days. The kids are often out the door in such a chaotic rush that the concept of sitting down together for breakfast seems farcical. But I did really enjoy it (and still do) on the rare occasions when it happens. We still make it a priority for birthdays and other special occasions.

I know that in many families the traditional evening meal is under threat. There seems to be much more competition these days than when I was a kid. Multiple sports practices, meetings, phone calls, the internet and TV seem to battle for precious family time. The sit-down evening meal is becoming less common as families grow in size and the demands on our time become greater. I think that sometimes we underestimate how important a meal shared with family really is. Not only is it a great chance to actually be together as a family unit (hopefully without too many distractions), but it is also a chance to systematically catch up on what everyone is up to.

In our house, we use this time to catch up on the news or achievements of the day. Sometimes we get pearls and other times we get nothing at all. But it's a great time to check in on what's happening and to see how everyone's going with life. We get a chance to chat about Exam results, excursions, dentist appointments, afternoon teas, brunches, Uni, jobs and anything else that may have occupied the day. The humble tea table is a training ground for our leaders of tomorrow. It's a place where our kids learn and hone the art of conversation and where they learn to share their news and their views. It's also a place where they develop listening skills. So, some level of chaos is inevitable. That's ok.

If you're managing to nail this aspect of family life, congratulations and keep it up. If it's a struggle, or you've developed bad habits, it's never too late to turn things around. Staying connected in a creative and intentional way doesn't necessarily mean that meal times are particularly ordered. Often, quite the opposite is the case. I don't want people to think that the evening meal in the Simpson household always goes to plan. Kids get up, sit down, disappear to who knows where (although we discourage this). Animals tend to run in all directions. Recently, the pet rabbit was on the loose and nibbling at our shoes under the table while we ate. Not the most relaxing meal time I've had. Have a think about some basic strategies (and boundaries) that will help to keep you on track. In our house the television goes off and there are no devices at the table. We do our very best to all remain seated for the duration of the meal (though this can be a challenge) and the phone can ring all it likes, t won't be answered during tea time.

Underpinning all this stuff is love. Love covers a multitude of family challenges and conflicts and spurs us on to keep working on family traditions and dealing with the inevitable rough edges. We usually mis-define love and replace it with something shallow and weak. The Apostle Paul provides us with the best definition of love I've ever come across. It's usually read at weddings, but it applies to absolutely every aspect of life. Take some time to study it and try your best to apply some of the characteristics that it identifies.

1 Corinthians 13: 4-7: *Love is patient and kind. Love is not jealous or boastful or proud or rude. It does not demand its own way. It is not irritable, and it keeps no record of being wronged. It does not rejoice about injustice but rejoices whenever the truth wins out. Love never gives up, never loses faith, is always hopeful, and endures through every circumstance.*

You'll have your own strategies for fostering family time around the dinner table. If they're good, stick with them. If they're lacking a bit, it's never too late to work on some new ones. Continue to develop and embrace the Corinthians definition of love. The more that you lean into these characteristics, the more chance you will have to maintain rich and fruitful family connections.

THE INCONVENIENT MONKEY

For a number of years when our kids were young, we would pencil in an annual snow trip. Each September, our family would venture to the Victorian snowfields. It was primarily a social event, a chance to spend a few days with close friends sipping lattes and throwing snowballs. If, however, the sky is blue and the snow plentiful, we have been known to hit the slopes for a day of boarding or skiing. It was always a magnificent time away and we looked forward to it every year. Packing the car and actually getting there was, however, a massive undertaking. I recall one particular trip for all the wrong reasons. Our initial estimated time of departure on this occasion was 1.00 pm. I had some misgivings about this as I wanted to leave much earlier. But one thing led to another and by the time we left it was much closer to 6.00 pm. Not ideal.

We stopped on the Hume Highway at Wallan McDonalds for tea. The kids mucked around on the playground while Lara and I struggled with the ordering process. It's never straightforward. I wouldn't be at all surprised if the poor girl behind the counter resigned after this experience. We chopped and changed and then deleted items and then upsized and downsized and changed drink flavours. At various stages the kids came and went and everyone had something constructive to add. Lara has a very mathematical brain. She visualises all kinds of things in her mind's eye. Maths people are all the same. Just because they understand it, they expect everyone else to as well. So, she places these incredibly complex fast-food orders and wonders why the 15-year-old kid on their second shift doesn't follow what she's ordered. By the end of this particular order, we just had to eat whatever arrived on the tray. Nobody could complain because nobody (apart from Lara) actually had any idea what had been ordered. Even then, there had been so many additions, deletions and up-sizes that I think even Lara was a little perplexed.

William (our third child) had decided to bring his beloved stuffed monkey into Maccas to share the experience (this was quite a long time ago!) I didn't pay too much attention to this. We ate, we drank and then we set off again up the highway. As we hurtled along in the dark, I heard whimpering from the back seat. To my great disappointment, I was informed that the stuffed monkey had been left at McDonalds. I couldn't believe this. It seemed to happen wherever we went. William was extremely attached to the monkey. It was a gift presented by Lara and Hannah upon their return from an overseas trip to China. I really had no choice but to make my way back to the Golden Arches.

I eventually found a spot to perform a very questionable U-turn. Not the easiest thing to do in the dark on the Hume Highway. I then had to drive back past Maccas and perform another questionable U-turn to get back to where the beloved monkey had been left. It was a twenty-ish km round trip. Not the end of the world, but to be driving in the opposite direction to your destination some 7 or so hours after I had planned to leave home was frustrating to say the least. The monkey was eventually found piloting the helicopter at the very top of the playground. Relief for all involved.

It struck me that life is chock-a-block full of frustration and inconvenience. No matter how well you plan, things always seem to arise that force you to change, moderate or adapt your plans. Families, friendships, jobs and colleagues can all create inconvenience. I've come to realise over the years that it's actually really important to accept inconvenience as a natural part of the daily routine. When faced with it, you can either lose your cool or just roll with it. There are occasions when you have no control over inconvenience. Maybe your train is late, you get a flat tyre, a tradesman does a no-show or a plane is cancelled. You can't control these external circumstances. But there are plenty of others that you can control. There are lots of times when you need to allow yourself to be inconvenienced for the sake of others. These are sometimes tough calls because they demand putting the needs of others ahead of our own wants and desires. This is about going the extra mile.

Jesus had some interesting ideas on what it meant to be inconvenienced for the sake of others. It was counter-cultural then and it is counter-cultural now. It certainly has the capacity to create some challenge, pain and even awkwardness. In the most famous sermon of all time, Jesus lays out a bit of a blueprint for how we should live our lives. It's about the best framework for harmonious and intentional living that you're ever likely to come across. It's not an easy life, but the results are likely to be otherworldly. Matthew 5 v 39-47:

> *But I say, do not resist an evil person! If someone slaps you on the right cheek, offer the other cheek also. If you are sued in court and your shirt is taken from you, give your coat, too. If a soldier demands that you carry his gear for a mile, carry it two miles. Give to those who ask, and don't turn away those who want to borrow. You have heard the law that says, 'Love your neighbour' and hate your enemy. But I say, love your enemies! Pray for those who persecute you! In that way, you will be acting as true children of your Father in heaven. For he gives sunlight to both the evil and the good, and he sends rain on the just and the unjust alike. If you love only those who love you, what reward is there for that? Even corrupt tax collectors do that much. If you are kind only to your friends, how are you different from anyone else? Even pagans do that.*

I love it when I see people allowing themselves to be inconvenienced for the sake of others. Many of us do this very well. It does, however, take a fair bit of practice to get right. It's not the easiest thing to do. May I encourage all of us to look for opportunities to be inconvenienced. Put yourself out for someone else and do it with the best attitude you can muster. It will sometimes involve a bit of frustration and some huffing and puffing. Take a step back and have a look at the bigger picture and you'll see how important and rewarding it can actually be.

UNFINISHED HOUSE

Throughout their high school years, my kids have generally relied on public transport to get to and from their school. It usually consisted of me dropping them at the local train station, where they board the trusty "stopping all stations" heading for Flinders Street. I'm a bit of a softy though. I actually loved driving them to school. I took to driving them more frequently following the pandemic. Driving them to school has proved to be a time of great connection, deliberation, debate and sharing of ideas. This has been even better since I declared that the use of mobile devices on the way to school was an offence. As a result, we have spent many hours "people watching" and providing social commentary on what unfolds around us. Over the years, I became the passenger and instructor as each of my kids obtained their L plates. While there have been some terrifying moments, to date, we've never exchanged any paint with other vehicles.

Depending which route we take, we often travel past some very fancy houses. There is a stretch where the houses are truly extraordinary. We've watched many of the old ones getting knocked down over the years. In their place, we've looked on with interest as an array of Greco-Roman and French Provincial Mansions have taken their place. These new houses are adorned with massive columns and bespoke doors, windows and gates. They are amazing.

I was always a bit sad when I drove past one particular unfinished project that sat there looking very despondent. This two-story mini mansion sat in its sad and unfinished state for well over 10 years. It was recently knocked over and the only reminder now is a vacant block with some barely visible foundations. I often thought about what it must have represented to whoever started the project all those years ago. The unfinished and dilapidated house screamed of a lost dream. No doubt this project had been dreamt up by some proud family. But, for whatever reason, things had turned bad. I often think about what happened to the individual or family who had the dream of living there. I wonder where they are now and whether or not they are still plagued by the loss of their dream home. I'm possibly overthinking this.

On one level, I suspect that most of us have unrealised dreams in our midst. Perhaps now more than ever. Most of us don't have to think too hard to identify missed opportunities or major disappointments. Maybe it's a career move that didn't turn out the way we'd envisaged. Maybe it's a relationship that fell apart without warning and there was nothing that you could do about it. I've experienced this. It's painful. Sometimes the loss of a close relationship is so painful that it's intoxicating. It can dominate your thoughts as your emotions oscillate between sadness, anger, disappointment, frustration and grief. And even when you muster as much optimism as you can, you still can't envisage how restoration will ever happen. Perhaps it won't.

When Covid-19 arrived in all its fury, none of us had to try very hard to identify some shattered dreams. So many students were robbed of all those rites of passage like final school camps, formals, the building of camaraderie, sports days, school plays and "normal" valedictory celebrations. My boy Charlie did year 12 during 2020. He had months off school as Victoria was in Covid lock-down. He missed everything. Even his 18th birthday ended up as a small gathering on Zoom. As parents, we all want the very best for our kids. We want them to experience all the good stuff that life offers. But often these things are out of our control. There is a certain helplessness when we experience the crashing of our dreams or those missed opportunities. In many cases, they are impossible to get back. We just have to deal with them.

So, that's the challenge. How do we deal with shattered dreams and missed opportunities? I'm no expert. I've experienced a few in my time. I know this much. I try to worry about the things that I can control and not about the things I can't. I concede that this is easier said than done. But a positive attitude and outlook is super important. A focus towards what you have rather than what you don't is also a great strategy. I think that it's all about perspective and gratitude. Disappointment is ok and even normal. In fact, it's important to name our losses. When we name them, we can grieve over them. You can even have a cry if it makes you feel better. But then it's important to look at all that you've got. If you've got access to safe drinking water, you're better off than 2.2 billion others. If you've got access to safely managed sanitation services, you're better off than 4.2 billion others and if you have basic hand washing services, you're better off than 3 billion others.

If you're experiencing a season of shattered dreams and disappointments, let's do our best to keep things in perspective. Have a think about what you can do to be part of the solution for others who are experiencing fundamental and life-threatening unrealised dreams and lost opportunities. It's also important to keep in mind that being a follower of Jesus does not guarantee us an easy road forward. But it does offer each of us the great comfort that despite everything, God is in control and Jesus wins! I often think about this verse in Habakkuk. It's my go-to when things start to get the better of me. I trust that it's a comfort and encouragement to you too.

Habakkuk 3 v 17-18: *Even though the fig trees have no blossoms, and there are no grapes on the vines; even though the olive crop fails, and the fields lie empty and barren; even though the flocks die in the fields, and the cattle barns are empty, yet I will rejoice in the Lord! I will be joyful in the God of my salvation!*

WHEELER DEALER

I n the weeks prior to Christmas one year, I decided that I wanted to buy my boy a new BMX bike. I scoured eBay but couldn't make anything work. I then started trawling through the web pages of local bike shops. I found one that stocked a massive range of BMX's. I'm a bit of a BMX snob and I had quite specific ideas about what I was after. Like any consumer, I wanted the best bike for the best price. My eyes lit up when I found a website that stated that they accepted trade-ins! You little beauty! I rang up the store and told them what I was after. They confirmed they had one in stock AND also confirmed that they would take a trade-in on this bike.

Before setting out for the bike shop, I rummaged to the back of my garage and found an ancient (not in a collectable sense) BMX. It had two flat tyres, shredded hand grips and over time rodents of some description had gnawed away at the seat. The paint and stickers had faded and it was not pretty to look at. I stuffed it in the car and hurried over to the fancy and well-stocked bike shop. Upon arrival, I struck a rather serious looking man. If he wasn't the owner, he certainly gave the impression that he was a man of some importance. This was perfect. Hopefully the trade-in scheme had been his brain child. He probably raised it at some marketing meeting. I thought to myself that he would be more likely to honour the store policy than some kid with baggy pants and a backwards cap.

I chose the bike that I wanted and then casually informed him that I had a trade-in stashed in the back of my car. As we walked out to the car, I explained that it was quite a special bike and that I wouldn't be letting it go cheaply. I think that I captured his interest. After all, everyone has a bit of "American Picker" in them. I threw open the sliding door and produced this horrendous excuse for a bike. He just looked at it in stunned disbelief. I tried to keep it serious. I said I was happy to compromise a little on price on account of the fact that he would have to put his own air in the tyres. He didn't know what to do. To cut a long story short, we found ourselves haggling at the counter. We eventually shook on a deal. He would give me 5 bucks if I promised to take it home again. DONE DEAL!

Just like the shiny new BMX, the old busted BMX was once a treasured possession. It was probably given as a present to a young child. It may have been ridden around on Christmas day in years gone by. But now it was broken and faded. I have been reminded in recent times how unimportant material possessions actually are. We all like having nice stuff. That's OK. But real treasures lie in things like friends, family and a sense of peace and contentment.

In the New Testament Jesus has a lot to say about earthly possessions. In Matthew 6 v 19-21 Jesus says:

Don't store up treasures here on earth, where moths eat them and rust destroys them, and where thieves break in and steal. Store your treasures in heaven, where moths and rust cannot destroy, and thieves do not break in and steal? Wherever your treasure is, there the desires of your heart will also be.

So, it's important to try to keep your eyes on what really matters. Surround yourself with people who bring out the best in you. Churn your time, effort and energy into things that have eternal value and try not to get side-tracked by the mundane and irrelevant. It's all about perspective and sometimes it helps to step back and make an assessment of what you've got, what you need and what's important.

SNAPPY DRESSER

I spend plenty of time sitting in foyers of suburban Magistrates' Courts. I've worked as a criminal Barrister for over 25 years. As a Barrister, I appear for individuals and companies who have been charged by the Police and other agencies with a wide range of offences. It's a great opportunity to meet all kinds of people who have found themselves in a variety of predicaments. It's certainly never dull. Not only do I get a chance to meet the client, but inevitably I meet their partners or parents or other close connections. This can, at times, be quite entertaining. Courts are always interesting places. They are not the kind of places that everyone wants to find themselves. In my experience, most people find the experience of going to court quite nerve wracking.

The majority of people make some kind of effort to "style up" a bit for a court appearance. Despite my total lack of personal styling, I do sometimes provide styling tips to those who ask. My tips are not extensive. No footy shorts, take out your obvious piercings (if possible), cover your major tattoos, and wear a neat and tidy shirt (preferably with sleeves). There is a happy balance somewhere between activewear and a tuxedo. That's usually what I recommend. For some, this means a three-piece suit and faux crocodile skin boots. For others, it's high viz and the snazziest jeans they can find. I once saw a bloke inside a courtroom wearing a baseball cap and holding 2 Mega 7/11 Slurpees - one in each hand. This probably wasn't the best look in the circumstances. It's also quite hard to open and close doors with both hands accounted for. Just saying.

On another occasion, I saw a bloke whose massive arms were covered in tattoos and wearing a reasonably snug black T-shirt. It wasn't his massive tattooed arms that caught my attention (though they were pretty impressive), it was the slogan emblazoned on the front of his shirt. It simply said, "Don't be afraid to fail." While I probably wouldn't be donning this Tee for a Court appearance, I love the sentiment behind it.

While it seems that things hadn't worked out so well for this particular defendant, nobody can criticise him for having a go. He'd made a blunder of some kind and there he was at Court facing the music. Actions and consequences.

I speak to so many people whom I know, that are not living the way that they want to be. I'm talking about normal mums, dads, friends and neighbours. They aren't achieving the goals they once had and they are reluctant to go about setting new ones. These people still do ok, but they seem to lack contentment or peace or possibly both. You probably know people like this. Maybe you're one of these people. Maybe it's your partner or one of your parents or even one of your kids. The reason that so many people don't actually end up doing what they really want, or being who they were designed to be, is because they are just too scared to fail. Most people start their journey with curious minds and loads of potential but they don't like to make mistakes. As we all know, this isn't limited to children. If anything, it can get worse the older we get. While some of us are naturally risk averse, others of us get more conservative as the years tick by.

Don't get me wrong, there's a time and a place for caution. Things can (and often do) go terribly wrong for those that rush in. But there are certainly times when we all need to focus on the positive outcomes, achievements and accomplishments without being bound or overshadowed by the risk factors and the fear of failure. If Sir Edmund Hillary was too scared to fail, he'd never have conquered Mount Everest and if Neil Armstrong exercised too much caution, he would never have bounced on the moon.

Spend time at some stage putting yourself under the scope. What needs to change? What have you been putting off because you're terrified of mucking it up? What areas of your life do you need to re-jig? Are you happy with where things are for you? What steps do you need to take to achieve your goals or at least commence plodding in the right direction?

It's not too late to adjust your gaze and look toward a slightly more adventurous and rewarding horizon. And, "Don't be afraid to fail."

2 Timothy 1 v 7: *For God has not given us a spirit of fear, but of power and of love, and of a sound mind.* (NKJV)

TABLE FOR 3

Many years ago, a lovely lady organised a food roster for our family. For the 2 weeks following the birth of our first child Hannah, various people arrived on our doorstep with wondrous culinary creations. Until you've experienced this, it's difficult to appreciate exactly how valuable it is. The roster was (almost) seamless (more of that in a moment) and operated with very limited fuss. People would turn up, deliver something yummy and then graciously retreat back down the path. The fascinating thing about this process is that we didn't actually know anyone on the roster. They were complete strangers, known only to the lovely lady who put the roster together. This was a very humbling experience.

There was one evening, when the sun had set and the curtains had been drawn. We waited and waited and nobody arrived. I began contemplating a home cooked meal (possibly toast or noodles). We were not unaccustomed to cooking for ourselves. We had done this successfully for years. But, when you've been the recipient of nightly deliveries, the cupboards were not as well stocked as they could have been (this was well before the phenomenon of Uber Eats). As I was sitting there scratching my head, there was a knock at the door. Standing on our front porch was a 20 something year old girl with multiple bags of Thai takeaway. Don't get me wrong, I love lasagna as much as the next bloke. But the sight of take-away Thai made my heart beat a bit faster. On this occasion, however, instead of the usual custom of dropping and running, she just said "hi" and stood there. After a moment or two of awkward silence, I invited her inside. She wasn't in a hurry. So, she came in and sat at the kitchen table. The logical next step was to ask whether she'd already eaten. She hadn't. And so, we invited her to join us as we ate her Thai takeaway at our table. She was very pleased to join us.

For the next 30 minutes or so, we smashed down some spicy Thai treats with a complete stranger. It was quite a unique experience. She chatted away about this and that and we asked her about her family and her job. I don't remember her name, or where she lived or anything at all about her actually. And I've never seen her since. If you'd like to give it a try, sit down with a random family at your local food court. Engage them in conversation and see how it pans out. Not quite the same, but you get the drift. It took all my conversational skills to keep this dinner date on the rails. But we got there in the end.

Hospitality is a funny thing. We all know people that do hospitality so well. Their homes are open and they are always ready to entertain. For others this is a real struggle. It's usually connected to the kind of house that you grew up in as a kid. If your own parents had an open-door policy, chances are that you will probably have one yourself. The opposite may also be the case. There is no right or wrong with this stuff. However, I think that we should all try to be as welcoming and hospitable as we can. Make room in your world (if you can) to look after the needs of others. Invite people over, leave your front light on, be generous to friends and strangers alike.

In the same way that we were blessed by an unknown 20 something female all those years ago, it's important to think about ways to bless and be generous to those around you. It's important to actively look for opportunities to improve the well-being of those within your sphere. Whether that means inviting your neighbours in for a BBQ, baking someone a cake, washing a car or baby-sitting for someone who needs a night out, the possibilities are endless.

The Apostle Paul, in the book of Galatians outlines the characteristics of the Holy Spirit. These are the things that we often see in the lives of those who are doing their best to live like Jesus.

Galatians 5 v 22-23: *But the Holy Spirit produces this kind of fruit in our lives: love, joy, peace, patience, kindness, goodness, faithfulness, gentleness and self-control. There is no law against these* things!

Work out what kind of family you want to be. Whether you're married or single, whether you've got kids or not, do your best, with God's help to always demonstrate these wonderful characteristics. The more that you demonstrate these to others, the more likely it is that they will start to rub off on those around you. Be the one to set the standard in your neighbourhood, workplace, sporting club or family. Don't be at all surprised if your actions inspire others to do the same.

KING OF THE MOUNTAIN

I know that not everyone in the world builds their social calendar around the Bathurst 1000 V8 Supercar race at Mt Panorama. But most people would know that the Bathurst 1000 does hold a pretty significant place in the Australian psyche. It is a 1000 km race around one of the greatest and most demanding race tracks in the world. It takes place in Bathurst NSW. A single lap of the race track is a distance of just over 6 km with long straights, tight corners and a very steep climb as well as a steep descent or two. To race this circuit for 1000 km takes roughly seven hours. This race never disappoints. It's a wonderful day of thrills and spills that always keeps me glued to the TV.

On two occasions I've made the pilgrimage to Bathurst, NSW for the race weekend. This was in the early 1990's. I camped on top of the Mountain with mates and it was rowdy to say the least. Back in those days there wasn't much in the way of control and the nightly activities were characterised by lots of heavily bearded men behaving badly. There were plenty of high-octane antics with seemingly little concern for property or self-preservation. The highlight was a massive dust bowl surrounded by literally thousands of people. Cars would spontaneously appear and perform figure 8's and donuts within metres of the cheering crowds. To spice things up, people would then throw burning toilet rolls at each other as well as at the cars. It was a bit like a grown-up version of dodgeball. It was both terrifying and exhilarating to watch and the behaviour and antics were dangerous in the extreme. The sights, the sounds and the smells that go with a weekend like this remain deeply etched in my psyche. I'm told that they have now set up a family camping area. I'd probably stay there if I was ever to take Lara and the kids. Surprisingly, Lara has never expressed any deep interest in joining me on such a venture! Strange.

At the end of racing each day we were allowed on the hallowed race track to walk a lap. It is only when you do this that you actually get some perspective about what a gruelling race track Bathurst really is. It's hard to pinpoint the ingredients for success at Bathurst. Those who win the great race usually do so because everything goes right for them on the day. It is a race of endurance that requires impeccable preparation, a hugely dedicated and professional pit crew, a very experienced team manager, a very wealthy team owner and a spectacular driver. Improvisation, sound decisions and a good dose of luck doesn't hurt either. Race drivers don't enter races to come last. Everyone enters with the hope that they will finish the day standing on the podium.

In one respect, success in life is not dissimilar to an assault on Mt Panorama. There is usually no one single factor that sets us up for a successful/satisfying/prosperous/happy life (if these are in fact your goals). Regardless of what goals we have for ourselves and our families, it is inevitable that achieving them will depend on a whole range of variables. We need to identify the different factors that are operating in our own lives: our friendship group, our job (paid or unpaid), our level of disposable time, our finances, our support networks and our priorities. All these things are part of our reality and each of them will have an impact on the goals that we set for ourselves and our families. While there are plenty of things in life that we can't control, there are also lots of important things that we can. My suggestion is that you should identify the things in your life that you CAN control and set about controlling them. Running off the track every now and then is ok. In fact, it's inevitable.

Keep your eyes on where you're heading, follow the advice of those that you respect, pace yourself, make adjustments as you go and expect the unexpected. Remember that pit stops are an imperative part of the journey and if you don't make regular and scheduled times to evaluate, assess, reflect and recharge, you'll find yourself in all kinds of bother. Take time to look after yourself and those that you love and remember that you don't have to win the race on the first lap. Patience, determination and consistency are what is needed to come out a winner.

In the first book of Corinthians the Apostle Paul also talks about life in terms of a race.

1 Corinthians 9 v 24-27: *Don't you realise that in a race everyone runs, but only one person gets the prize? So run to win! All athletes are disciplined in their training. They do it to win a prize that will fade away, but we do it for an eternal prize. So I run with purpose in every step, I am not just shadow boxing. I discipline my body like an athlete, training it to do what it should. Otherwise, I fear that after preaching to others I myself might be disqualified.*

It's pretty good advice from a man who knew a fair bit about determination, challenge and hardship. Think about the ways in which you could incorporate this wisdom into your everyday life. It may just change your outlook.

A MONUMENTAL BLOKE

A number of years ago I was introduced to a bloke through a good friend of mine. This guy had a very colourful past. He'd been in lots of trouble in his younger days and had spent his fair share of time in and out of jail. He lived in Pentridge Prison well before it was full of latte sipping yuppies looking for their first townhouse. Those were the bad old days. He told lots of colourful stories which usually ended with him being apprehended in dramatic style. By the time that I met him, things were going much better for him. He'd cleaned up his lifestyle, got himself married, started a business and bought a house. I've since stayed with him and his wife. Not a stolen item in sight!

Many years ago, when he was broke and reckless, he owned a V8 Fairlane. This immediately appealed to me. When I hear V8 and Fairlane in the same sentence my ears prick up. I've had a couple over the years and they truly are a magnificent car. Large, thirsty and powerful. What appealed to me about this story, however, was not the fact that he simply owned one. Rather, it was the fact that he learnt to drive it in a very unique way. He jumped in his Fairlane one day and discovered that he had a major problem with his automatic transmission. It would only engage reverse gear. Since he was broke (and reckless), he decided to simply "make do." In all other respects the Fairlane went well. So, he took to driving it everywhere in reverse. He did this for a number of weeks. Over that time, he became so accomplished at driving it backwards, that he was able to rely entirely on his rear vision mirrors. So, unlike the rest of us that look over our shoulder when we reverse, he could drive flat-out backwards while seemingly looking forwards. This is the stuff of action movies – Fast and Furious eat your heart out!

The funniest thing about this activity is that he also learnt to indicate and overtake vehicles while going backwards. He told me that he derived great pleasure from doing this at high speed on busy freeways. It's not something that I'd recommend and a prolonged commitment to this style of driving is likely to end in tears. But this bloke would pull out and pass other cars going backwards but facing forwards. I imagine that this would be quite off-putting for the person driving in the traditional manner.

We can learn a lot of lessons from what's behind us; lessons about human nature and about the communities in which we live. We can learn about our families and we can look at what others have achieved or failed to achieve. All these lessons from the past can then point us in the right direction and can help to shape our future. In the same way that driving backwards can be a dangerous pastime, living with our eyes and attitudes behind us can also greatly hamper our ability to live a positive and balanced life. We've all got stuff in our past that impacts how we live and the decisions that we make. Some of it may be really positive, but some of it can bind us in crippling ways. Maybe your childhood was difficult and painful. Perhaps those who should have loved you and protected you actually generated misery and sadness.

We've all got a choice to make. We can look at the sadness of the past and perpetuate that in our own lives and the lives of our families. Or we can make a conscious decision to break the chains of the past and make our own lovely chain for the future. For some this is easier than others. But with the right help and the right outlook and attitude, there's no reason why the sadness in the rear vision mirror should continue to dictate how we live our lives in the future. There's absolutely no reason why we can't all set about building a positive, loving and stable future for ourselves and our families despite the baggage from the past. If your history is dictating your future in a negative way, ask for help. Breaking chains isn't easy, but it's worth the effort.

I love stories of transformation and the story of this client was one of the best I've come across. When I appeared for him at the Heidelberg Court, I told the Magistrate about how much his life had changed. The Magistrate himself actually described this as a story of redemption. His words - not mine. I love that.

Paul the Apostle reminds us in 2 Corinthians 5 v 17:

Anyone who believes in Christ is a new creation. The old is gone! The new has come! (NIRV)

It's a classic reminder to each of us not to be defined by who we were, but by who we have become by God's grace.

MUSCLE CAR MANIA

'm the middle of three boys in my family and we all love cars. While I always tinkered with cars more than the other boys, we all loved and appreciated cars in all sorts of shapes and sizes. Our Dad was largely responsible for this life-long affliction. He was a Baptist minister with a love affair with big cars (mainly Cadillacs) of which he's had three.

As teens and young adults, my brothers and I had a passing parade of relatively cheap but interesting vehicles parked in our driveway. We had everything from Cadillacs to Morris Minors and even a rotary powered Mazda R100 (should have kept that one). At one stage the vehicle count reached 13. This was a reasonably big number for a regular house block in the suburbs. On one occasion, one of Mum's friends popped over and thought twice about coming in because she didn't want to disrupt the party. She was stunned to find Mum home by herself. The cars parked in the driveway and strewn across the front lawn were just spares.

In the early 1990's we lashed out and bought ourselves an original 1969 XW GT Falcon. This was a pretty serious car. These things were built to go fast and it did that pretty well. It came out on sunny days and usually attracted a fair bit of attention. I recall one afternoon in late 1993, Triple M 105.1 (a local radio station) had a promotion that the first 105 cars to the local BP Petrol Station would get a free tank of petrol. Together with my younger brother Luke, we fired up the GT and rumbled it down to the servo in question. We lined it up with all sorts of other hopefuls wanting a top-up. Most of them were driving sensible 4-cylinder Japanese cars.

One of the interesting features of the GT Falcon was its petrol tank. It had the "Bathurst" 36-gallon tank (164 litres) which was standard in the GT Falcons of that era. On that particular afternoon the tank was low and I managed to squeeze 152 litres into it. This almost put a stop to the promotion there and then. Having filled it up, I went into the shop to get my name ticked off. The bloke behind the counter made a public announcement: "No more GT Falcons!" This outing was a true unexpected gem in an otherwise very normal day. We brought the GT home and syphoned petrol into all the other cars. It was a great day out.

We've all heard stories about things that turn out badly. The newspaper is full of hard luck stories about the best laid plans that often fail. However, I'm sure that all of us can also tell stories about experiences that have turned out much better than we ever anticipated. Perhaps you've had a stay in a hotel and you've been given an unexpected upgrade, or you've been given a jazzy hire car when you asked for the cheapest available. Maybe you simply drove to the shops on a wet day and were lucky enough to get a pole position car park.

The reality is, that it's easy to dwell on the things that don't go quite right. I suppose that we need to balance these experiences against the unexpected gems that pop up from time to time. It is all a matter of attitude. That's not to say that we can't moan and groan a bit when things turn out badly. That's a part of life and we don't have to pretend that we live without disappointments. For those with a Christian faith story, it's important to remember that God is our protector and our place of refuge. Even when life derails, we can rely on the absolute promises of God.

Psalm 91 is a remarkable and wonderful Psalm. It's a Psalm about God's amazing protection for those who love Him.

Psalm 91 v 1-4: *Those who live in the shelter of the Most High will find rest in the shadow of the Almighty. This I declare about the Lord. He alone is my refuge, my place of safety; he is my God, and I trust him. For he will rescue you from every trap and protect you from deadly disease. He will cover you with his feathers. He will shelter you with his wings. His faithful promises are your armour and protection.*

We sold the GT Falcon in about 2000. It seemed like a good idea at the time. On average it has appreciated in value by about 50% each year for the last 20 years. DOH! Had it still been in the shed it would be worth a small fortune. I guess that's life.

THE RULES OF BOWLING

A number of years ago, I headed out with a few mates for a night of 10 pin bowling. I bowled a bit as a kid. It was pretty hard to get through primary school in the 1970's and 80's without being invited to a 10-pin bowling party. In my experience, bowling is something that you enjoy as a kid, then put down for 10 years or so. You then pick it up again in your late teens or early 20's. It's often a favourite destination for a first or second date. You then take your kids there when they are around 10 or 12 and then you usually venture back to bowling in your early 50's to try and recapture your youth and try to prove to yourself (and others) that you've still got it. However, in your early 50's is when your bits and pieces start to ache. In this age bracket, bowling is an activity that requires careful management. I'm in the latter category. I've probably only bowled 3 times in the last 15 years. In preparation for this outing with my similarly aged man-friends, I decided to get on the internet for a few pre-game tips. I quickly discovered a website that told me absolutely everything I needed to know about bowling. This site has tips on everything from where to buy a retro bowling shirt to essential bowling etiquette.

With no time to waste I headed straight for the section that told me how to bowl my best game ever. This was exactly what I needed. Good, solid, no-nonsense advice. In a nutshell, this is the advice that it gave:

1. Pay attention to your character
2. Develop self-awareness
3. Control your emotions

Are they serious! I just want to know how to knock down the pins. I'm not after a psychological assessment. I want strikes, spares and absolutely no gutter balls. I was in a hurry to show my mates the extent of my raw natural talent. I simply didn't have time for all this emotional stuff. For me, bowling is a bit like golf. Regardless of how often I play, I usually do about the same each time. A few gutter balls, a few strikes and the odd spare. That's pretty much how I go. I'll probably never buy my own ball and I think a personalised retro bowling shirt is out of the question.

However, the three pointers (let's call them the "bowling rules") may actually come in handy for something else. As I read them, I immediately thought of how relevant they were to the art of developing, maintaining and nurturing our relationships with others. Most of us can think of a relationship that we've mucked up over the years. Or maybe we can identify a failed relationship that someone else mucked up for us. Either way, we've all had a relationship or friendship of some kind that has taken a nosedive. In my experience, it is much easier to blame the other person when a relationship or friendship fails. Maybe it's justified and maybe it isn't.

Regardless of the cause of the breakdown, I think that as a society we are generally reluctant to analyse our own conduct when things go bad. It's much easier to blame. I think that if we are to develop, maintain and nurture lasting relationships we do need to consider our own actions and emotions. Rather than making value-judgements about others, maybe we can think about our own responses. Rather than having an outburst when we feel wronged, maybe we can think about ways to react that will save us the trouble of getting all worked up. If we spend time identifying how the 3 "bowling rules" apply to our own lives I think that each of us will be much better equipped to deal with the complexities that can characterise our interactions with others. Part of this is being able to identify and name those areas in our lives that we need to work on. If we lack insight about our own shortfalls and rough edges, it's actually very hard to change our tune. This is especially so if a relationship needs us to be proactive in trying to reconcile.

Sometimes we can rely on those around us to work on this stuff. However, this won't always provide the answers that we're looking for. The Bible says that we can actually talk to God about this stuff. Psalm 139 v 23-24 says:

Search me, O God, and know my heart; test me and know my anxious thoughts. Point out anything in me that offends you, and lead me along the path of everlasting life.

So, there it is – God is interested in the little details of our lives. It's ok to ask him about stuff that we don't even understand ourselves. By the end of the night, we had two games. I slipped over once and bowled a gutter or two. A good night was had by all. As for the "bowling rules," I'll certainly use them, but probably not at the bowling alley!

HIDDEN TREASURE

've always been interested in stuff. I like all kinds of junk. The more unique the better. I'm drawn to trash and treasure markets and swap meets in particular. I love cars, classic mini-bikes, petrol bowsers, garden art, pinball machines, old signs and classic push bikes. So, when a mate told me about an ancient bike shop near me that was closing down, I couldn't get there quick enough.

This was no ordinary bike shop. We entered via the rear yard. There were bikes and bits of bikes absolutely everywhere. There was over 40 years of junk lying around the place. It was like an episode of American Pickers and it was awesome.

I was slowly making my way through the maze of busted bikes in the rear yard towards the shop itself, when my junk collecting comrade emerged from the back of the shop with a look that said, "Get in here NOW!" And that's just what I did. The shop was in a total shamble. Stuff everywhere. Old, new, dusty and rusty. I couldn't believe what was crammed in there. There was decades of history stuffed in that little shop. Relics from a by-gone era were standing side by side with flashy new bikes of all colours and sizes. But what grabbed my attention was neither flashy nor new.

Standing amongst the sea of chrome and steel was a classic 1970's dragster. It was the kind that Bobby Brady used to ride (for those that watched the Brady Bunch). Most people who went to Primary School in the 1970's would have been presented with one of these Dragsters for a Christmas or birthday present. My older brother Andrew and I were each given a Dragster on Christmas morning in 1976. We rode these bikes for years and we both still have them. The bike that I spied in the ancient bike shop had full length mudguards, a chrome sissy bar, massive handlebars, a banana seat and a T-bar gear shifter mounted between the seat and the head-stem. What excited me about this bike was that it was brand new. It had sat in the shop since the 1970's.

Nobody had ever bought it. It conjured up wonderful memories of Christmas 1976 when I was presented with my own dragster. I couldn't believe my luck. First thing was to ring the Minister for Finance. I had not come prepared for such a purchase. I spoke to lovely Lara and did my best to explain what I had found. I found myself babbling like a little school boy. She had no idea what I was talking about but graciously gave me the green light. What a woman!

After a bit of haggling, a deal was struck and the dragster was mine. I brought it home and showed it to my family. They had trouble connecting my excitement levels on the phone with the bike that I wheeled in. No, it wasn't a new-new bike; it was a new-old bike. Anyway, it all made complete sense to me.

So, this old bike had sat there as floor stock for the best part of 40 years. By the time the BMX craze started in the early 1980's, nobody wanted a daggy old dragster. And there it sat. It had experienced its moment in the sun and now the sun had set. It was yesterday's news and had become easily overlooked. The newer models overshadowed it and it was just pushed to the side to make way for the latest and greatest.

Have you ever felt like this? Do you sometimes wonder why opportunities seem to keep passing you by? Do you feel like you've lost your MOJO? I speak to so many people who struggle with their own perception of who they are. Plagued by self-doubt, insecurity, anxiety and depression, so many people have actually forgotten how valuable they really are. It's so easy to find yourself going down this road. Each of us is fearfully and wonderfully made. We are not an accident and we each have a task to fulfil. If you find yourself feeling under-appreciated, overwhelmed and failing to measure up, it's time you started taking steps to turn this around. Friends, family, workmates, neighbours, your local GP and your local church are good places to start. It's super important to just start the conversation with someone. Don't gather dust for any longer than you already have. You and I both know that somewhere under the dust lies a treasure just waiting to shine again.

In Ephesians, the Apostle Paul says the most remarkable thing – He describes each of us as "God's masterpiece." How radical is that?! Some translations describe us as God's handiwork. We are created in God's image and he is desperately proud of each of us.

Ephesians 2 v 10: *For we are God's masterpiece. He has created us anew in Christ Jesus, so we can do the good things he planned for us long ago.*

So, not only is God incredibly proud of you, but he's also planned in advance things for you to do. He has set a calling in the heart of each of us. We are not random accidents. We are God's precious creation and he wants to journey with each of us in a profound and unique way.

HOT WHEELS

My Granny died in 2018, just before her 97th birthday. She was an amazing woman and she was fit and active right up until she died. She was a godly lady and she showed an active interest in her large family until the very end. She had 4 children, 8 grandchildren and 15 great grandchildren. She built an incredible legacy and maintained a sense of fun and enthusiasm her entire life. She was community minded and she volunteered in the local opportunity shop until she was 95 or so. We miss her. We all counted ourselves as very fortunate to have GG (Great-Grandma) as part of our wider family for such a long time.

We did, however, have to ban her from driving when she was in her early 90's. This decision was made in response to a driving display very similar to something you'd see at Movie World or Universal Studios. The major difference was that Granny's stunt driving ended in her car being towed away after her special trick. It was sad for her, but a relief for the wider community. Anyway, after she stopped driving, I had been trying to think of ways to keep her mobile. One of my very charitable neighbours loaned me a mobility scooter. The sole purpose of this was to give my Granny a little taster. What I wasn't anticipating was how much fun these things actually are. If you haven't tried a mobility scooter, do yourself a favour. Ring up your great Aunt, Uncle, Grandma, elderly neighbour (whoever) and offer to do their shopping for them. Moments before you leave, tell them that your car has a flat tyre. Then ask boldly if you could possibly borrow their scooter. No, don't do this. But think of a way of getting a turn. You'll never look back.

William, Gracie and myself drove it over to Granny's for a brief demo. Granny did have a drive and while she seemed to enjoy it, she didn't feel super confident in it. We decided to let her think about it for a while. Following our visit, myself and the kids decided to go for a few laps of the block. I'm serious when I say that I considered selling my car and just pimping up one of these. I could justify the numerous laps of the block on the basis that I had a twinge in my knee. However, long-term, the mobility scooter would be difficult to justify. The kids, however, started dreaming up ways to raise money and there was even discussion about how the popularity stakes would rise if you could ferry your mates to high school and back. My daughter Gracie (who chalked up lots of kilometres with me) was so keen. As I tucked her into bed that night, we discussed the various ways of making this work. She immediately began thinking about effective fundraising strategies. I bumped into a bloke at church the following day who asked with some hesitation, "Is there any chance I would have seen you crossing the road on a mobility scooter?"

While I jest about the fun of the mobility scooter, for plenty of people, these are a crucial link to the outside world. They offer the opportunity for less mobile people to get out and about and to connect with their friends and their community. For many, frailty or something else keeps them much closer to home. It struck me that there must be lots of lonely people tucked away in homes right through the community. I was shocked to read recently that the highest age-specific suicide rates in Australia for both males and females was in the 85 years and over group. With this in mind, we've all got a role to play in trying to make our community better places. You don't have to save the world with this one. This is a chance to look much closer to home. Have a think about where you live. Maybe it's the person across the road, down the street or over the back fence. You don't have to reinvent the wheel. Look for opportunities to involve them in a few family activities. Invite them in for a cuppa or offer to mow their lawn. Drop in some home-made cookies or a DVD that you think they might enjoy. I know that some people are sensational at this. If you're a bit nervous, start small and see how it goes. You might be surprised at the wisdom and friendship that is ready and waiting where you least expected it. The Apostle Paul has the following to say about living lives committed to others:

Galatians 6 v 7-10: *Don't be misled – you cannot mock the justice of God. You will always harvest what you plant. Those who live only to satisfy their own sinful nature will harvest decay and death from that sinful nature. But those who live to please the Spirit will harvest everlasting life from the Spirit. So let's not get tired of doing what is good. At just the right time we will reap a harvest of blessing if we don't give up. Therefore, whenever we have the opportunity, we should do good to everyone – especially to those in the family of faith.*

THE WHEELS ON THE BUS

The Simpson family haven't always been into caravans and camping. When I was a young, I looked at caravans with a certain level of scorn. My parents never owned one and (as far as I'm aware), never contemplated buying one. I viewed them (caravans, not my parents) as being slow and cumbersome. I never understood why any family would tow an ancient (and usually daggy looking) caravan for hundreds of miles when most holiday destinations had perfectly serviceable accommodation already there. Of course, with four kids of my own, I developed the view that we couldn't really live without one. I look back on my pre-caravan days and can scarcely believe how naïve and unpatriotic my views actually were. Caravans are an entrenched part of our Australian identity. How un-Australian of me.

So, when the kids were small, we lashed out on an ancient (and daggy) caravan. It was an old Jayco pop-top. It was an eBay special and was purchased sight-unseen. It was in NSW (about 8 hours from us) and it wasn't practical to view it prior to purchase. So, we parted with our cash, found a few clear days, packed up our people mover and made the long journey up the coast to meet it for the first time. We were given an induction by the vendors before setting off on a 5-night caravan holiday back down the coast to Melbourne.

This little van served us well and it became our home away from home. We eventually outgrew it. In February 2011 we took delivery of a 40-year-old Bedford school bus. My parents bought it in the mid 1990's. It used to belong to U.S. Bus Lines in Belgrave, Victoria. It was a route bus in the 1970's. It is now decked out as a motorhome. It is modest but comfortable. When we got it, it was very slow and at times quite frustrating to drive. It had no air conditioning and no power steering. But it was part of the family and we loved it. Over the years, we have taken this old girl all over the place. It's had a few updates now, including a 454 Chev V8, air-con and power steering. We love our time in the old Bedford (affectionately named Bustin' Loose) and it can be a bit frustrating waiting for the next set of holidays to arrive. Even when holidays do arrive, they are often jam-packed with all manner of other commitments. What to do?

It was time to think creatively. Late in the afternoon on one particular Saturday, we packed up Bustin' Loose and set off. We headed East on Whitehorse Road to Ringwood. We turned right at Eastlink and started heading south. We took the Wellington Road exit. We then re-joined Eastlink and headed back towards Ringwood for a few hundred metres. And just like that, we reached our new favourite holiday destination: the BP Roadhouse on Eastlink (only 18 km from home). We headed straight for the truck parking area, and there we stopped, in amongst the interstate trucks that were resting for the night. While a petrol station road-house is traditionally reserved for a coffee stop, petrol and brief toilet break, we managed a great deal more. We had McDonalds for tea. We talked, played a game, had a hot chocolate and then bedded down for the night. We all had a lovely sleep before heading back home in the morning. I would call this a mini-break. It was terrific family bonding with a real holiday feel all within 18 kilometres of home! Even the dog enjoyed it.

This unconventional mini-break showed me that the basic things in life can sometimes be the most memorable. We didn't spend much on this particular outing. The destination was far from extravagant and the planning was minimal. The objective was time together as a family. This we achieved in spades. The kids still talk about it and will probably look back in years to come and wonder whether their parents were in need of some professional help. Nonetheless, it is easy to let small but important memory building opportunities pass us by. While I'm not suggesting that camping on the side of a major freeway is for everyone, there are plenty of things that families can do to build traditions and memories without breaking the budget or taking annual leave.

The Bible is full of stories about families and about family traditions. Abraham, Isaac, Jacob, Joseph and David all had lives that were steeped in family traditions. Traditions, however, are not as commonplace in society these days. While ancient families operated very differently to ours, it was the family unit where things happened.

I love to hear stories about families setting off for a local adventure. I'm sure that many of you do these things already. If you do, keep the good times rolling. If you don't, now's the time to start planning your own family adventure. Keep it short, simple, inexpensive and creative. Your kids will love it.

One of my own little family traditions (that doesn't cost a cent) is to say a simple blessing over my kids every night. I've been doing this since my kids were quite young. Even now, I still take the opportunity to bless them whenever I can. Our kids need as much help as they can get. I'm a firm believer that a simple blessing on them before bed can bring them richness, protection and peace. Even when they're away, I'll say a blessing over their empty bed or at their doorway. The opportunity to say a blessing draws on thousands of years of Biblical tradition. The Priestly blessing that I say over my kids, dates back to the Jewish traditions of the Old Testament where God instructed Moses to get his brother Aaron and his sons to bless the people of Israel. This blessing is still practiced today in Jewish synagogues and communities. I say a variation of the blessing found in Numbers 6 v 24-26. While this varies across the different translations, the specific wording that I say over my kids (and their friends if they happen to stay over) is as follows:

May the Lord bless you and keep you. May the Lord make his face to shine upon you and be gracious unto you. May the Lord lift up his countenance upon you and give you his peace.

YOU GOTTA LOOK THE PART!

I used to play a bit of golf as a teenager. I picked the clubs up again in my early 20's before having a reasonably lengthy hiatus. My absence from the courses of Melbourne and the Mornington Peninsula was not a great loss to the golfing fraternity. I was never a good golfer. I managed to get onto the occasional good drive, but generally speaking, I wasn't much good. I quite liked the social aspect but I was unlikely to ever win a "closest to the pin" competition. It's a strange game. The more I played, the less consistent I seemed to be. I certainly didn't detect any difference in my game regardless of how frequently I played. When I was in my mid 30's, I was invited to have a round with my mate at his private club. I instantly knew I would play exactly the same way as I had approximately 10 years earlier. On reflection, I suppose that I was reasonably consistent. Just not in the way that most people want to be.

This private club was pretty fancy. It was one of those clubs where you just have to say "I'm with him" and point to the bloke in your group who has the jazzy clubs and the membership. I'd never played at a private club prior to this and so I wasn't absolutely clear about golfing etiquette. But I tried my best not to look totally out of place. I failed miserably.

Unfortunately, my choice of clothing fell somewhat below par according to the gentleman in the pro shop. Not only did he not like my shorts (they were the closest thing to tailored shorts that I owned) but he didn't like my choice of socks either. I couldn't believe this and I felt quite affronted. I'd actually tried to look as golf-pro as I possibly could. So, what to do? We retreated to the car park for a few minutes and engaged in a bit of mixing and matching. If our wives could have seen us, I'm sure they'd have been impressed.

We set about trying to find a dress combination that not only fitted but also received the approval of the golf pro. I ended up wearing my golfing host's socks (white ones this time) and shorts. My host scrounged a pair of long pants, a belt and another pair of socks to replace the ones that I was now wearing. There were a few tense moments as the clothing switcheroo took place – Why don't they have change rooms in the carpark? I wonder if the club has a suggestion box?

When we appeared back at the pro shop, I was looking much more like a golfer. The major problem was that my gracious host had a slightly more streamlined physique than me. So, while I managed to get his shorts on, I found myself having to walk like the Tin-man from the Wizard of Oz. Despite my various limitations (both my skill level and my clothing related mobility), we had a fabulous time. This was just the tonic at the end of a busy day.

It's funny that while my golfing clothes made me look more like a golfer, they had no discernible positive impact on my game. This reminds me a bit of the old saying, "it's what's on the inside that counts." There is a strong temptation for all of us to get caught up with outward appearances. Whether it is physical looks, the car we drive, the house we live in, where we go for our holidays or even the clothes that we wear. Don't get me wrong, I don't think there is anything wrong with taking some pride in all of these things. We just need to realise that when we examine ourselves and others, it is the hidden treasure that lies within that really counts.

I love the story in the Old Testament when Samuel turned up and anointed a very young not-yet-coronated King David. He was directed by God to visit Jesse and his myriad of sons. As Jesse lined up his eligible sons, Samuel was pretty impressed with what he saw. 1 Samuel 16 v 6-7 is a classic:

When they arrived, Samuel took one look at Eliab and thought, "Surely this is the Lord's anointed!" But the Lord said to Samuel, "Don't judge by his appearance or height, for I have rejected him. The Lord doesn't see things the way you see them. People judge by outward appearance, but the Lord looks at the heart."

As it turned out, David was just a shepherd boy. Jesse didn't even bother dragging him in to meet Samuel until Samuel asked if there were any other sons. I'm sure that this would have created surprise and confusion among Jesse and the boys. It's funny how God works.

During my time at the swanky private club, I lost a stack of golf balls and spent lots of time walking adjacent to the fairway, this was all just part of the experience. Good weather, great company and a bit of exercise at the end of the day. It doesn't get much better than that.

JUST FOR FUN

Most people who live in Melbourne have been to Luna Park at some stage. It's a fun-park on the city fringe with something for everyone. The last time we went there, the kids took a couple of their mates along and everyone had a superb time. It was beautifully clean and the attendants were friendly and well dressed. There was that familiar and rather enticing smell of the cinnamon doughnuts hanging in the air. There were lights and mirrors and music and the sounds of children having fun.

I always feel a bit nervous when I go to any amusement park that has a big dipper. I undergo this internal struggle of fear versus excitement. If I was absolutely sure that a carriage would not derail mid-ride, I would embrace the experience without hesitation. But I've never been to an amusement park (and I've been to my fair share) that has signs telling you that their rides are 100% safe. On the contrary, there are usually signs that try and talk you out of going on their rides. I find these a little disconcerting.

Pregnancy, recent surgery, back, shoulder or neck pain or a heart condition are generally listed as ailments that will have any would-be funster grounded at an amusement park. At any given time, I could usually fulfill most of these categories. I don't need much of an excuse to keep my feet on the ground. It is, however, pretty difficult when the kids are tugging on your arms to keep them company.

On this particular excursion to Luna Park, it was with some fear and trepidation that I joined my kids and lined up for a turn on Luna Park's famous scenic railway. It sounds relaxing, doesn't it? It's a very quaint looking ride. It has a really traditional roller coaster look about it. It's made of wood and the carriages are highly decorated and painted in bright colours. Interestingly, it even has a gripman that stands in the middle of the ride pulling a big handle backwards and forwards to control the speed. It reminded me very much of the famous cable trams in San Francisco. It was a similar concept, but it just went about 10 times as fast. The Scenic Railway has a rich history. Luna Park prides itself on the fact that its own Scenic Railway is the oldest continually operating roller coaster in the WORLD! It was built in 1912. Don't get me wrong, I like old stuff. I like old cars, old houses, old people, and I have a love of history. For me, however, I prefer my thrill-rides to utilise cutting edge technology.

When I strap in for high-speed entertainment, I like the thought of a ride that has been designed by NASA. At the very least I would like it to share some common components with the new RAAF Strike Fighter. Maybe I'm in the minority on this. The lines for the Luna Park Scenic Railway seem to confirm that I'd missed the point. I ended up having plenty of turns on the beloved Scenic Railway and I have to say that it's a real hoot. It's still fun even by today's standards. I can't imagine what sort of blast it must have been for those who were riding it in 1912.

The Scenic Railway taught me that age and a sense of history can be just as important and entertaining as any new fandangle ride. It's not just about going fast and getting a super smooth ride. The Scenic Railway is the full package. It has charm and provides the user with a unique glimpse into another era.

These days we all seem to spend most of our time thinking about the future. We think about what we are going to do next week, next year and next decade. Where are we going to live, what car are we going to own and how much are we going to earn? It's OK to think about these things. But it doesn't hurt to have a look at what we can learn from the past.

In the book of Jeremiah, we are provided with some wonderful advice. Jeremiah 6 v 16 says:

This is what the Lord says; "Stop at the crossroads and look around. Ask for the old, godly way, and walk in it. Travel its path, and you will find rest for your souls."

I encourage all of us to think about a world where bigger, faster and newer is not always best. Consider an era when dependable, predictable and reliable were highly valued. Take the opportunity to learn from the wisdom of your elders, be they grandparents, neighbours or family friends. Be on the look-out for spiritual wisdom from those who are further along the path than you. A long Christian heritage is a great blessing. But if you haven't got that in your own family, don't panic. A borrowed Christian heritage is totally fine. Find a family, a pastor or a close friend and learn the lessons of God's faithfulness from them. Stories of faithfulness are so important. Learn from them, celebrate them and tell others about them.

WORSE THAN CHILDBIRTH!

During the many years that I worked as a school chaplain, I would spend two full days per week on-site at the local primary school. I recall one particular day when I mucked around in the playground at lunchtime and then spent some time in the classrooms with the little kids learning their names. It was a reasonably big school and there were lots of names to learn and master. It wasn't always easy, but I came to appreciate the power of a name. At the very end of this particular day, I felt a little twinge in my lower back. By the time I got home and played a couple of games of chasey with my daughter Gracie, the twinge turned into a dull throbbing pain. By about 4.30 pm I was downing the Nurofen. The pain came and went in waves. I slept ok but by 5.30 am the next morning, I was in all kinds of bother. What to do in a situation like this? Of course, I turned to my old mate Dr Google. I felt that some self-diagnosis was called for.

Lower back pain, nausea, and abdominal spasms. I was either in labour or I had kidney stones. After a few key word searches, I determined that it was more than likely the latter. I scoffed a few more Nurofen and put on my suit. I had a court appearance that morning that I couldn't easily shift. I secured the services of Lovely Lara as my chauffeur and desperately tried to get on with my day. This was no easy task. If you've ever had kidney stones, you'll know exactly what I mean. I only just managed to keep things together and I kept telling myself that pain was just a state of mind. When presenting a case in Court, the etiquette is to stand up. It's just as well, because I was completely unable to sit. The pain was extraordinary. After my Court appearance, I hobbled back to the car and Lara drove me home again. I just about needed a walking frame by this point!

Early in the afternoon, I managed to see a doctor. I told him about the self-diagnosis I had made. He did not immediately concur. To be on the safe side, he organised a CT scan. Expensive but definitive.

I had two kidney stones and a renewed enthusiasm for the power of Google. I have since discovered that kidney stones are rated higher than childbirth on the pain ranking scale. I'll be tucking that little gem away to pull out when the timing is right. Where would we be without the internet? The pain ranking scale looks at the ailments that people experience and ranks them according to their pain levels. One assumes that in order for this to be an accurate ranking, a particular individual will have needed to experience childbirth, pancreatitis, kidney stones, gallstones, a broken femur, a dental abscess, third degree burns and a heart attack. I'm not sure where they'd find the time to work and raise a family with all these things going on.

In any event, my kidney stones were small but painful. Do you have things in your life that are small but painful? Perhaps you have things that started as something small but somehow grew into something much bigger. Maybe an argument or some hurtful words with a friend or family member that was never resolved. Maybe you were hurt by the words or actions of someone and you've never managed to let go of them. These sorts of things can eat away at you over time and become your reality.

I read a book once about what it means to love others. It talks about how love is not an emotion but a choice. Love is selfless and it is giving to another without any guarantee of getting anything back. It is giving to others what they need and not what they deserve. Real love requires knowledge, love and practice. This will be a revelation for many. It's about loving others just because. I recall the way that Lara and I loved our kids when they arrived in our lives. We loved them so deeply even though they didn't give us anything in return.

So, if you have something in your life that is either niggling you or downright painful, think about what you can do to try and change things. I'm not talking about physical niggles or pain. I'm talking about the emotional ones. What choices can you make to turn things around? You're never going to get along with everyone and there will always be people in your life whom you find hard to deal with. That's ok.

Sometimes, all you can do is to identify your common humanity. Maybe you have some kind of family heritage that provides some common ground for you. Do your best to identify your common ground and then look (squint if you have to) to see the good qualities in those people who otherwise present major challenges. Maybe all you can do is to make the decision to be courteous, generous and civil in your exchanges. Make the conscious decision to forgive. Not because the other person deserves it, or because they've even said sorry. Saying sorry actually has nothing to do with it. Regardless, it's still important to forgive whether it's for their benefit or yours. Don't carry stuff that you don't need to. Life's too precious to hold on to old hurts and pains.

The Apostle Paul provides a bit of wisdom on this stuff. It's worth considering and it's likely to help kick-start the process of rebuilding what is broken.

Colossians 3 v 12–13: *Since God chose you to be the holy people he loves, you must clothe yourselves with tender-hearted mercy, kindness, humility, gentleness, and patience. Make allowance for each other's faults, and forgive anyone who offends you. Remember, the Lord forgave you, so you must forgive others.*

AIR CRASH INVESTIGATORS

O nce upon a time, I turned my mind towards getting a new driveway at my house. I had a poke around on Google and found someone who looked as though they understood the art of driveway construction. After signing on the dotted line and parting with a healthy deposit, I waited and waited for my driveway man to arrive. After a couple of weeks, I thought that it was probably time to call and see whether he was still a trading entity. He assured me that he was and that he would shortly be commencing work.

Approximately 3 weeks later (5 weeks after I had paid my deposit – but who's counting) he arrived with his bobcat. We explained exactly what we wanted and he made all kinds of assurances and backed them up with sweeping hand gestures. I felt somewhat reassured that I had made the right decision. His parting words to me before I rushed off to school that morning were; "You won't recognize this place when you get home this arvo." Never a truer word was spoken!! Interestingly, I actually ducked home during the morning to pick something up. I arrived home at about 10.45 am. No bobcat and no driveway man. Instead, there was just a massive pile of stones and the most incredible muddy mess that I had ever seen. It genuinely looked as though an A380 had crash landed at the front of my block and skidded out of control in the direction of my back fence.

Not wanting to put him under undue pressure, I gave him over 2 weeks before I placed a call to see what his intentions were. He explained that it was wet and that his bobcat got bogged and that there was nothing he could do. All of this is probably true. I cannot say for sure. All I know is that 33 additional days then ticked by and there was still no sign of him. Lara kept telling me to just be gracious and she made all manner of excuses for him because he was "such a lovely man." She said that in the greater scheme of life, it doesn't really matter. To a certain extent Lara and I agreed to disagree about this. I had visions of him sunning himself somewhere and drinking expensive drinks while he laughed with his friends about this gullible bloke in the eastern suburbs of Melbourne.

Ultimately, it was really about a clash of expectations. I had an expectation that he would build me a driveway. Once the project stalled, I had an expectation that he would call me and explain what he proposed for the future. My expectations were totally unrealised. This had me both frustrated and disappointed. Mismatched expectations are a very complex issue and have the capacity to de-rail otherwise solid relationships.

I think that most of the relationship difficulties that we experience in our lives (and we all have them) have their roots somewhere in the sphere of unrealised expectations. Not only do we have to manage what we expect from others, but it is extremely important to understand and try to manage the expectations that others have of us. Oftentimes the expectations that we place on ourselves can be even more destructive and debilitating than anything anyone else could place on us. The difficulty is that our expectations are often totally unrealistic. When they go unrealised then it is very easy to feel hurt, misunderstood, undervalued and even a bit feisty. Most busted relationships have their genesis in unrealised expectations.

If we are sensible, honest and reasonable with our expectations, then we maximize our chances of being satisfied. In turn, if we communicate our own expectations appropriately to others then we also maximize our chances of satisfying others. Communication about our expectations is definitely the key. So, if you can identify relationships in your life where there is a clash of expectations (maybe with a colleague, a partner, a teenage son or daughter or a tradesperson), pluck up the courage and have a mature conversation about it. While it may seem awkward and scary at first, it's likely to make things easier as you move forward. It's super important, however, not to be too hasty or judgmental in your response to a difficult or frustrating situation. Even if you feel offended, misunderstood or un-heard, getting on the same page has often got more to do with listening and understanding rather than talking and directing. While there is certainly a place for clearly expressing your opinion and expectation, you should carefully evaluate the best way of going about this. It may be that you need to think carefully before having what may be a tricky conversation. The book of Proverbs is full to the brim with clever, wise and very helpful advice and direction:

Proverbs 18 v 13: *Spouting off before listening to the facts is both shameful and foolish.*

The driveway man eventually rang and said that he would soon be back. His communication settled my fragile and gullible heart. Work hard to understand the situation before "losing it." And, where possible, don't lose it at all. When you lose your cool, the only one that suffers is you.

SWIMMING BETWEEN THE FLAGS

Many decades ago, my Dad decided that he wanted a motor-home. On their honeymoon in 1967, Mum and Dad drove to Sydney via the coast in their 1957 Chev (they should have kept that one!) While they were in Sydney, they inspected a paddock full of Double Decker buses that had just been retired from active service in NSW. Dad desperately wanted to buy one. Very wisely he decided that such an impulse buy may have placed some unnecessary pressure on their brand-new marriage. Some thirty years later, the dream was still alive. Dad had talked about the missed opportunity of a Double Decker bus for years. So, in his early 50's, he ended up finding a retired Melbourne school bus that had been converted into a Motorhome. It was a classic old Bedford and it was painfully slow. But it provided Mum and Dad with many memorable experiences and lots of happy adventures. The old Bedford was eventually re-deployed for service in my little family. Lara and I made a few changes before setting out on our own adventures.

One of the most memorable was a 7-week road trip. We loaded up the (t)rusty old bus and motored up the east coast from Melbourne to Queensland. We eventually got as far as the town of 1770 (just over 2000 km from home) before pointing the bus in a southerly direction and moving slowly back toward home. It was a fabulous time spent together as a family. We had lots of adventures and we did lots of fun stuff. We spent a great deal of time swimming and boarding in the ocean. I have always been a bit of a nervous swimmer. Ever since I can remember, Mum would stand on the beach and yell, "Philip, that's far enough." She doesn't do it as much these days. However, I'm sure even now, if she joined us for a family holiday, she would still feel the need to stand on the beach and squawk in my direction. I tend to do the same with my kids these days. Whenever they challenge me, I just blame it on my overprotective Mother.

When we were at Coolum (on the Sunshine Coast) we swam on the beach in quite wild conditions. The wind was blowing and the waves were quite rough. We positioned ourselves in the centre of the flags. We always swam between the orange and yellow flags. On one occasion, I looked up into the tower, but I couldn't see anyone there watching the beach. I'm not sure whether they were there or whether they had ducked off for a mid-morning sausage roll. Either way, I still felt strangely reassured that everything was OK as we were swimming between the flags. In reality the flags weren't going to do me any good if there wasn't anybody ready and primed to save us should we all be sucked out to sea. That aside, I still felt safe. The mere presence of the flags offered me a certain level of comfort.

I'm sure that we all know someone who is currently experiencing some kind of personal pain or difficulty. Perhaps you have a friend that is sick or lonely or just plain sad. Maybe you know someone who is grieving about the loss of a loved one or the loss of a relationship. Whatever the problem, it is often hard to know what to say or do when we encounter these circumstances. I think the natural tendency is to want to solve their difficulties for them. This is understandable. Nobody likes to see a friend in pain.

It's perfectly ok not to give advice. In fact, it's often best not to. Oftentimes the most important thing you can do is to simply be a presence in their difficulties. There are times when words seem shallow and empty. It is, however, important to never underestimate the power of simply being available and present for a friend in need. Stand along-side them in their times of challenge. Shoulder the load with them and make yourself visible. Your presence and availability will often be of much greater comfort than anything you could possibly say.

If you find yourself wondering how to care for a friend in need, remember the little yellow and orange flags flapping by the seaside. While you mightn't solve their problem, your presence and visibility will likely be a marvellous encouragement and comfort.

In the book of Job in the Old Testament of the Bible, there is a story about Job's friends. Upon learning of the tragedy that Job had suffered, his friends travelled to his home to comfort him.

Job 2 v 12-13: *When they saw Job from a distance, they scarcely recognised him.... They sat on the ground with him for seven days and nights. No one said a word to Job, for they saw that his suffering was too great for words.*

In doing this, Job's friends simply practiced the presence. Unique but powerful, and something that each of us is capable of doing.

PLATES AND PICTURES

Most families I know have kitchen cupboards that house at least a few brightly coloured kinder plates. You know the ones I mean; our little cherubs carefully drew them when they were aged between 3 & 5 years old. They remain a classic fundraiser at kindergartens and preschools the world over I expect. I happen to love these plates. I did one or two myself when I was a kid. We love having friends over for dinner. I remember one occasion when we tried to be as fancy as our humble home would allow. We actually had a sit-down dinner!! The only "matching" set of dinner plates that we could find were our brightly coloured kinder plates. I say "matching" because they are all the same shape and size. I performed a stock-take and discovered that we had 22 of these plates. This was more than I expected and it represents many hours of creativity across a number of years.

Many years ago, when Lovely Lara and I celebrated our engagement, we were presented with a couple of very tasteful dinner sets. For a moment in time, we had genuine matching plates, cups and bowls. They are now just a distant memory. Over the years they were chipped, cracked, dropped, left outside or used for painting or feeding outdoor and indoor pets like dogs, cats, guinea pigs, rabbits and chooks. So, while we don't have many fancy plates in our kitchen cupboards, I'm actually super attached to our kinder plates. Each plate is unique and represents a moment in time for its creator. The plates also demonstrate the personalities and individual interests of each of my kids. They are covered in pictures of robots, flowers, dinosaurs, hand prints, family members, spaceships and a whole raft of pets long since committed back to the earth. We have actually just done another round of these plates. Despite our kids now being well clear of kinder, we used a few contacts to scam another round of these personalised plates. It was great fun and will add to our already impressive stash of personalised dinner plates.

If our plates were discovered in thousands of years, like the ruins of Pompeii, they would give a comprehensive pictorial history of what our family viewed as important and held dear. So, what's the point of all this ruminating? There was a time when my idea of a family meal included matching white china bowls. But my idea has changed considerably. Form has given way to function. Etiquette has given way to noise (and sometimes unruliness) and our current version of orderly eating would be shunned in all restaurants that use tablecloths (though things are much better than they used to be). As parents, we are frequently faced with competing interests within our families. Sometimes it is very difficult to know what to take a stand on and what to simply let slide. More often than not, I'm unsure which is which.

I know this much – children are a great blessing. There are times when they drive us totally bonkers. They bring out our short fuse. They test us and try us and have us pining for the "good old days." I'm sure this is normal. While we are all desperately trying to get it right, take some time to savour the faces and personalities that sit at your dinner table each night. While it's likely that your family has a few chips and cracks and non-matching pieces, take time to appreciate the variety, diversity, individuality and beauty that makes up your family. Guide them, direct them and set a positive example for them. Focus on the things that draw you together rather than the things that drive you apart.

In actual fact, it's the diversity that brings the richness. We're all different and we've all got our own personalities, gifts, skills and talents. Paul the Apostle in his first letter to the church in Corinth says the following:

1 Corinthians 12 v 12, 18-21 & 27: *The human body has many parts, but the many parts make up one whole body. So it is with the body of Christ. (v18) But our bodies have many parts, and God has put each part just where he wants it. (19) How strange a body would be if it only had one part! Yes, there are many parts, but only one body. (21) The eye can never say to the hand, I don't need you. The head can't say to the feet, "I don't need you." (27) All of you together are Christ's body and each of you is a part of it.*

No matter what gifts, rough edges, quirks and challenges are operating in your life, we all have a role to play and we are all created for a purpose. Work out where you fit and make room at the table for those around you as well. Only then, will you really discover the joy and power that comes from being part of a community.

MR CUNNINGHAM'S COINS

One of my great highlights of being a school Chaplain was Grandparents' Day. At my school we did this each year. I loved Grandparents' Day and I always liked trying to work out who fitted with who. It was always an impressive turnout and lots of people worked really hard to make this day a great success. In the lead up to Grandparent's Day one year, we talked a lot with the kids about the "olden days." I am often asked by my own kids what things were like in the olden days. How would I know? I'm not old! I suppose it's all about perspective. A number of years ago, when my firstborn (Hannah) was in Grade 2, she decided to take along to school a few relics from the days gone by. At that stage, we had a lovely senior citizen living next door to us. He got wind of this and he very proudly brought in a collection of old coins.

They were beautifully presented coins in a commemorative display book. The coins consisted of the full range of pre-decimal coins (pre-1966) together with the full range of matching decimal coins. They had been treasured by my neighbour for well over 40 years. We made all the right noises and admired them appropriately. He was eager for Hannah to take them to school for show and tell. I felt very nervous – it was a feeling of gratitude and terror all wrapped up into a single emotion.

We gave Hannah strict instructions about how to protect them on their journey to school and back. It was a highly prized show and tell experience and everyone at school was very interested in them. She brought them back home and we marvelled at our neighbour's generosity in letting them out of his sight. At that point we should have taken them straight back to him. I'm not sure why we didn't. We put them somewhere "safe" and got on with things, promising ourselves that we would give them to him next time he popped in.

The next time we saw the commemorative display book, it was being walked around the house by our then two-year-old, Gracie. By the time we wrestled it back from her, we made a very grim discovery. To our horror, the booklet was torn and our toddler's monkey-like fingers had removed most of the coins. "Where are they?" I screeched. Gracie led me to the ducted heating vent and pointed. She had posted the prized commemorative coins in various vents around the house. I was totally mortified. Most were never to be seen again. How does one recover from such a loss? I went through all the possible scenarios in my head. How would I tell my aging neighbour? He was in his 90's and I feared that this news may have been the end of him. Lara immediately jumped on eBay and managed to track down another set. Not that common we discovered. Didn't come cheap either, but it did the trick. We broke the news to our neighbour and presented him with the replacement. He seemed content with this arrangement. Not that he had much choice!

Grace prevailed and we remained firm friends with our neighbour. It could have gone another way though. It taught me an important lesson. When things don't go our way, it's easy to overreact. We've all done it. It would have been very easy for our neighbour to give us a caning. Heaven knows we deserved it. But he didn't. He accepted our apology and moved on. We received unmerited favour from him. That's what grace is all about. Undeserved but greatly appreciated.

In my experience, it's often the little things in life that lead to the breakdown of close friendships. When things are handled with grace, forgiveness and understanding the dramas that arise are usually no more than a blip on the radar. In the absence of such things, however, petty disputes can and do ruin relationships. A lack of understanding, a lack of perspective and the inability to swallow one's pride can spell the end of a friendship. Sadly, this story can be told over and over again. It's way more common than you might imagine, particularly within families. We all know families that just don't get on. Some manage to tolerate each other for the sake of "togetherness" on Christmas Day, while others have simply become strangers.

There's something about the dynamic of a family that seems to accentuate misgivings and grudges. Family disputes are the most painful and the most difficult to recover from. The reality is that many families simply never recover. This can entrench hostility, mistrust and judgement for literally generations. In fact, sometimes it will only be the subsequent generations that manage to "bury the hatchet" and agree to move on with the grace and understanding that their parents and grandparents couldn't muster. Look for opportunities to exercise grace and forgiveness to your children, your parents, your neighbours and your friends. You never know, when you're likely to need it yourself one day.

King David in the Old Testament understood the pain of broken relationships. He is described as a man after God's own heart. But he made his fair share of mistakes and felt the wrath and judgement of those whom he'd once been very close to. Psalm 55 is a Psalm that is full of anguish and pain. For those experiencing the loss of a precious relationship, the following Psalm will hopefully offer you some encouragement and comfort.

Psalm 55 v 12: *It is not an enemy who taunts me – I could bear that. It is not my foes who so arrogantly insult me – I could have hidden from them. (v13) Instead, it is you – my equal, my companion and close friend. (v14) What good fellowship we once enjoyed as we walked together to the house of God….(v20) As for my companion, he betrayed his friends; he broke his promises. (v21) His words are as smooth as butter, but in his heart is war. His words are as soothing as lotion, but underneath are daggers! (v22) Give your burdens to the Lord and he will take care of you. He will not permit the godly to slip and fall.*

CARAVAN ADVENTURE

I f you ask most people about the great Australian dream, it usually involves hitching up a caravan or camper trailer and disappearing up the coast somewhere. I know that there are many families that love the concept of life on the road. This lifestyle appeals to young and old alike. Whether it's a full lap of Australia or a few days sitting by the ocean or on the banks of a mighty river, we all love the idea of the free and easy lifestyle.

I met a guy a few years ago who decided to pursue his own (actually his wife's) caravan dream. His beloved wife decided that they should get themselves a caravan and join the ranks of the grey nomads. All her friends were doing it and she just loved the idea of a home away from home – one that you could take literally anywhere. My friend was not overly convinced by this. While he's made his share of rash and radical decisions over the years, he'd be just about the last person on earth that would regard a caravan purchase as a good idea. Not only would it fail his cost-benefit analysis, he's not particularly mechanical and is probably better suited to the hotel/resort style holiday than a caravan adventure. He'll sleep under the stars as long as there are 5 of them!

In any event, as often happens, the enthusiasm from his wife became almost intoxicating. He threw caution to the wind and bought a van. This thing was a massive family style van that was suitable for a full-scale family adventure. The fact that his kids were all adults did not deter his wife. She saw this massive van and she knew she had to have it. After the purchase, his wife spent many hours buying crockery and table-ware that was both colour co-ordinated and fashionable. Every detail of this van was appropriately planned, re-planned and tastefully executed by his wife.

The time came for their first adventure. This was to be a short trip from their home in the outer suburbs of Melbourne to a quaint little caravan park in Healesville. I've run this via Google Maps and it's a

37 kilometre trip. To cut a long story short, the maiden voyage was a complete disaster. Sadly, my friend had absolutely no idea how to back a caravan. Not only did he fail miserably when trying to park upon their arrival in Healesville, he then had to endure the anxiety countdown as he contemplated trying to back it out again when he packed up 2 days later. Both were monumental fails. He even had the proprietor of the caravan park offering special tips. All of this was to no avail. I'd like to say that this is a tale of persistence and resilience. I'd like to tell you that my mate is now the best caravan backer in the Southern Hemisphere. I'd like to say, they've consistently used their van for years and hardly know what they did before they got it. But this would be all lies.

Following their maiden voyage (a round trip of 74 kilometres), the big, beautiful, colour coordinated caravan was duly off-loaded at a $5000 loss. Never again was my mate going on a caravan holiday. It was an expensive lesson for an otherwise sensible and very capable man. I don't know too many other people that have spent $2500 per night on a caravan holiday. I think he and his wife both realised that such adventures would remain the domain of others.

I think the moral of the story is that we all make mistakes from time to time. We all act impulsively and find ourselves wondering how on earth we found ourselves in a particular situation. That is just life. But, we can all learn from the experiences of others. The great thing about being a part of a community is that we build up a certain corporate knowledge that can help us along the journey of life. Listening to others, learning from the mistakes of friends and neighbours and even sometimes proceeding with caution into new ventures and experiences can actually save you time, money and stress. While I'm a firm believer in trying new things, I've also learnt the wisdom of asking advice from others who are further along the path than I am.

Ecclesiastes 12 v 11 says: *"The words of the wise are like cattle prods – painful but helpful."*

Keep your eyes open, listen to sensible and timely advice and never stop learning. So, if you've got some decisions to make, or need to bounce some ideas, make sure that you knock on some doors and ask some questions. This will maximise your chances of making a good decision for yourself and your family. And if per chance you still make a blunder, it's unlikely to spell the end of the world as you know it. Learn from your mistakes and get on with things. And if you happen to have a mate who buys a large caravan on a whim and then develops buyers regret, do your bit to help him out. Make him an insulting offer and enjoy the colour coordinated designer crockery.

CHOOSE CAREFULLY!

L ike most parents, I spend a fair bit of time in my car. I'm either driving to work or dropping the kids somewhere. Whether it's driving the kids to school, dropping them at a sports practice or going to Saturday sport, I'm clocking up more kilometres than ever before. To pass the time on these journeys, the kids have developed a challenge. It's called "The car game." The idea is, that at any time between point A and point B, you need to choose the best car you can find and assume ownership. The challenge, however, is that once you've made your selection, it's locked in. For instance, if you get excited and lock in a Mini Cooper, and then you spy a Lambo or an SLS Mercedes, you're sunk! You are left to dream about what might have been.

It's interesting to observe the different approaches of my various children. Some are quick to lock in the first "fancy" car they see. Others (tending toward eternal optimism) will scoff at a Porsche Boxster in the hope that a new McLaren will cruise by. There are pluses and minuses of both approaches. The plus of biding your time is that you may just land the coolest car ever. The minus is that you may end up having to choose the minivan parked at the top of your street. I recall one Sunday evening when we were driving home from a family outing. Cool cars seemed to be in short supply. Each of us had locked in our choices before reaching the local McDonalds. Sadly, between Maccas and home we saw a Bentley Convertible, a Maserati and a brand new Lotus. Doh!

While choosing exotic cars is just a bit of fun, the decision-making process is akin to many other far more important decisions that life throws at us. We're all faced with options and choices in life. Oftentimes the pathway is unclear and the various options seem to look remarkably similar. When circumstances present themselves it's difficult to know whether to jump or to sit and wait for a better option. Sometimes it's a lesson in delayed gratification, avoiding the quick solution and waiting for a far more rewarding and fulfilling opportunity. Or alternatively, going with the safer and more familiar option to avoid the possible disappointment of losing out altogether. Naturally, there's risk associated with both approaches. This dilemma arises all the time. Whether you're looking to buy a house, searching for a job or trying to work out a course of study, it's not always easy to know exactly which way to jump.

I often find myself writing a mental or physical list when faced with these kinds of choices. Lists help to organise thoughts and a list of pros and cons is a great way to get a visual of what's at stake. Once a list has been written and dissected, it's important to gather information, investigate, scrutinise and analyse. Once you've worked out the facts, it's a good idea to also bounce the information off someone that you respect. Look at people in your life that you regard as good decision makers. Good decision makers are usually quite easy to spot. They are sensible, wise and established. Good decision makers usually make good decisions in all aspects of their lives: finances, relationships and pastimes. Talk over your options with a person like this and be prepared to have an open heart and mind. A teachable spirit will get you a long way.

In the book of Proverbs in Chapter 3 v 21 – 24 it says: *"My child, don't lose sight of common sense and discernment. Hang onto them, for they will refresh your soul. They are like jewels on a necklace. They keep you safe on your way, and your feet will not stumble. You can go to bed without fear, you will lie down and sleep soundly."*

So, there you have it. As a mate of mine once said, "It's not rocket surgery!" Despite the mixed metaphor, I trust that you've got the basic idea.

ALL THAT GLITTERS

O ne of my favourite (and most tiring) aspects of being a School Chaplain was going on school camps. For many of the years that I was a Chaplain, I went to three school camps per year. All told, I went to 27 school camps. Sleep deprivation ruled supreme. While I missed being away from my own family, I loved watching the kids have fun and I enjoyed getting to know them in a more informal setting. In the early days, we took the Grade 5 kids to an urban camp in the Melbourne CBD. With a spectacular line-up of parents and teachers (including a very affable and hilarious policeman), we packed up our bags and headed for Franklin Street, Melbourne. Our home base for our three-day stay was back-packer style accommodation nestled just a few steps from the Queen Victoria Market. It really was a very unique and interesting destination for a school camp. Over the course of the three days, we visited all manner of interesting attractions spanning the length and breadth of the CBD. Unfortunately, on this particular camp the heavens opened and dumped about 3 months of rainfall on us in 3 days. This makes for some fond memories! I recall at one point cramming 60 or so kids into a food court while we ordered each of them a hot chocolate. It was actually even more difficult than it sounds.

The first Melbourne attraction that my group visited was the Melbourne Museum. At the Museum we saw bugs and animals and even a 3D movie. The Museum was also packed with some mildly educational displays. I suppose this is essential these days for any school related activity. I think the kids would have preferred dodgem cars or mini-golf. Alas, as part of a special "goldrush" display, there was a special set of scales that measured your body weight according to its value in gold. It was quite an interesting exercise. According to these very special scales, I am worth $5,838,243.00 (give or take depending on the gold price). The kids got on and off the scales over the course of our visit. They were generally interested in being able to see what their dollar value might be should they suddenly be transformed into gold statues.

The question of value is a very interesting one. Not long after this, one of my own kids asked whether I would ever sell him, and, if so, how much would I be asking? While the thought has crossed my mind from time to time, I've always resisted the temptation. Depending on his behaviour at any given point, the price would fluctuate wildly. In the end, however, we decided that no price tag would be sufficient. The golden scales got me thinking about how we measure the value of ourselves, our friends and our family. On one level we can do some calculations based on how much a person can earn and contribute. We can look at their basic productivity and try to estimate (in dollar terms) what the value of their work/job/task may be. But these calculations are inadequate when we are trying to measure the worth of an individual as a friend, partner, child, parent or neighbour. These are the things in life that cannot be quantified in dollar figures.

If a loved one stood on the Melbourne Museum scales, we could establish their "gold value." Depending on their size, it would be enough to buy a nice house in a very leafy street. You're likely to have some money left over for a snazzy European car as well. If they were made of gold we would cherish and protect them. We would treat them very carefully and we would pay them the highest level of attention, knowing that we were protecting our investment. How much better should we be treating those in our life who are not made of gold? Our friends and families are likely to be the most precious and valuable resource that any of us will ever have. We need to make a conscious effort to demonstrate in both words and actions how much we really value them. Tell them this on a daily basis. Don't ever leave a loved one in doubt about exactly what they mean to you. And, should they (by some very bizarre occurrence) suddenly turn into gold bullion, then depending on their basic size and shape, you probably won't have to work again!

Remember that each of us is of awesome value. Despite the way that we sometimes feel about ourselves and others, the Bible is clear that we are valuable and precious. In Psalm 8 we are reminded of how valuable we all are in the eyes of God:

Psalm 8 v 3-5: *When I look at the night sky and see the work of your fingers – the moon and the stars you set in place – what are mere mortals that you should think about them, human beings that you should care for them? Yet you made them only a little lower than God and crowned them with glory and honour.*

It's a great reminder – Imagine that, God made us only a little lower than Himself and crowned us with glory and honour. Don't ever forget it.

EXPENSIVE PIANO

When my parents sold our childhood home, they needed to downsize some furniture. They had lived in the same street for 30 years. And then, in their 50's, Dad accepted a call to be the Pastor of a small Baptist church in Portland, Victoria. It was a pretty radical move at a time when many couples their age were counting their superannuation and assessing their retirement plan. Not my Mum and Dad. They were thinking well and truly outside the box. They always have.

So, we scored their old piano. It sat in our back room for a while and then after some re-shuffling, we decided that it should be moved to the front room. It's only 15 or so metres away – just down the hall. But, if you've ever tried to move an ancient steel framed piano, you'd know that this is a challenging task. So, I called a piano guy. The piano needed to be tipped on its end and moved through a doorway or two. The piano guy told me that he moves all sorts of pianos: from pianos worth close to $2.00 to pianos worth hundreds of thousands of dollars. I probably don't need to tell you which end of the scale my piano lives on. Anyway, he told me that the most expensive piano he had ever moved was a "Fazioli." I'd never heard of a Fazioli. But a quick check of the internet revealed that they have a rather nice showroom in Milan. The entry level piano starts at around $85,000 and runs through to about $400,000. The particular Fazioli that my piano guy was requested to move was worth a cool $320,000. The stunning aspect of the story was that the owners of this particular piano didn't even play! At least now they have a major incentive to start some lessons.

I got to thinking about what it would be like to have a $320,000 piano and not be able to play anything. Very frustrating, I think. A little bit like owning a new Ferrari without a driver's licence. The piano itself possessed all that potential for art and creativity and yet its owners did not have the ability to turn that potential into a beautiful sound. It's bad enough when this is said about an expensive object like a piano. But it is even worse when it can be said about a person. I often hear people talked about in terms of their potential. Potential is a good thing. But if it only ever remains potential then the potential loses its power. I see so much wasted potential. For all sorts of reasons, I see people who are brimming with potential getting themselves side-tracked or missing the track altogether. Pride, anger, addiction, poor decisions, ambition (yes ambition) can all contribute to people losing their way and missing what they were born to do. It's tragic.

As I look around my community, I see potential everywhere I look. I see people who have the potential to make a major contribution to their school, their community, their church and even their country. I see potential sporting champions, potential public leaders and potential academics. Some have an understanding of their potential and others are still searching for theirs. Either way it doesn't matter. What matters is that once you recognize your vast potential, then you need to get on with the job of developing it. If you're not sure how to, then ask a teacher, friend, pastor or mentor. If you're good at spotting potential in others, encourage them to develop their potential and be the best person they can be. Make the most of life and avoid being like a lavish and beautiful and silent piano.

Ephesians 1 v 4-5: *Even before he made the world, God loved us and chose us in Christ to be holy and without fault in his eyes. God decided in advance to adopt us into his own family by bringing us to himself through Jesus Christ. This is what he wanted to do and it gave him great pleasure.*

Judith Simpson 14 May 1947-10 September 2023

This photo was taken in January 2021 – It sums Mum up perfectly. In this photo, she'd just whipped up a fresh batch of scones for the Portland Beach Mission team. Mum was a servant. She loved others through radical and on-going acts of service. Nothing was ever too much trouble.

Life is worth the living, just because He lives

A lot has happened since I completed my first draft of this book. In mid 2023, I forwarded a printed copy of my draft to Dad. As a former English and social studies teacher, I figured that he was well qualified to cast his eye over my work. In doing so, he highlighted a myriad of grammatical faux pas and punctuation catastrophes. Once he completed the corrections and handed the papers back, I sat on my hands for months. In their typical way, Mum and Dad were very encouraging of my work. They enjoyed reflecting on the memories of some of the little stories that are now part of Simpson family folklore.

I can see it now. Mum and Dad would have sat happily by the roaring fire in their little farmhouse chatting away together. They would have compared notes and shared memories that ranged from profound to hilarious, such was our household when we were growing up. As Dad read my manuscript, Mum would have been quilting – something that she absolutely loved to do. She would have been sitting in her special chair surrounded by fabric and quilting projects, an array of little notebooks containing her handwritten lists and reminders. Her Bible would have been on the armrest. They would have been watching the footy or one of their beloved Gaither DVD's. The wind was probably roaring outside. It does this in the western districts in winter.

A lot has happened since then. In fact, it's been probably the toughest year of our family journey so far. On the morning of 10 September 2023, I woke to the buzzing of my mobile phone. It was some-time after 3.00 am. I prefer not to have my phone by my bed overnight. But the kids had been out with friends and when this happens, I like to keep the phone by the bed in case a car breaks down or something else happens. As I picked up the phone, I saw that it was a call from Dad. These are the calls that you dread. A call at this time of the morning is unlikely to be good news. I answered the phone and said "Are you ok Dad?" His answer came quickly, "Not really, no." I asked "what's happened?" He simply said, "Mama's gone to be with Jesus."

I actually couldn't process this news. Everything just stood still. Nothing about what he was telling me was making sense. I'd spoken to them the previous day. Mum had a cough, but she was improving. It had been a normal Saturday afternoon. They'd had friends at their house for tea. Mum had shown her typical hospitality. They'd chatted by the fire while Mum had quilted in her favourite chair. Nothing was untoward or unusual. Later in the evening, after their friends had left, she was having some trouble with her breathing. Dad telephoned the nurse-on-call. They recommended an ambulance. The ambulance attended their little farm. It's about 15 minutes out of town. After assessing Mum, the paramedics decided to take her to the hospital for observation. Dad said that he would gather a few things and told Mum to ring when things had settled. For reasons that we still don't really understand, Mum died on the way to hospital.

This news was totally unexpected and overwhelming. As dawn was breaking, we woke our four kids and let them know. This was tough. They loved their Mama. We were still in disbelief. This was truly unchartered territory for us. We hurriedly packed the car and made the 5-hour trek to see Dad. My brothers Andrew and Luke did the same. The weeks that followed were a bit of a blur. An emotional roller-coaster. The best way to describe my own response to Mum's passing is emptiness. No long good-bye. No hug, no kiss. No chance to laugh about the good times. She was gone. No more phone calls, no more home cooked meals in her wonderful country kitchen. No more chatting about life, kids, footy, food, ministry, quilts or holidays. No more opportunities to just sit with her and Dad or snooze on the couch as she pottered around their little home.

We are all still trying to come to terms with the loss. It's been way harder than I ever anticipated. Seeing Dad lose the love of his life has probably been the most difficult aspect of all of this. They were quite literally joined at the hip. They were life partners in the true sense. Their worlds revolved around serving Jesus together. Mum had died just over 3 months shy of their 56th wedding anniversary. Since her passing, we've had a whole list of firsts. Mum and Dad's first wedding anniversary without her, the first Christmas, the first New Year's Eve, Mum's first heavenly birthday, Mother's Day, Father's Day and Dad's 80th birthday. It's been a pretty tough journey for everyone.

It's interesting that when someone precious to you dies, the mundane and pedestrian become sacred and profound. Mama's quilts have become just about the most precious thing on earth. We've all been rationing her famous jam as though it is the most expensive and precious jam on the planet. Even her little bits of paper containing her beautiful handwriting have become keepsakes. Small reminders of a lady dearly loved. But Jesus loved her more. I'm actually writing these last few words while sitting in Mum's favourite green chair at their little farm. I always feel peaceful and content when I sit here. I can still hear her raucous and wonderful laugh when I sit here. She was a woman of passion and kindness and absolutely everything that she did was in the service of her God and others.

I've had a couple of dreams about her since she died. I count these as a great blessing. The one that sticks in my mind is a memory that I hang onto. Mum loved to sing. When we were kids, she sang a lot with her sister Lesley. They sounded wonderful together. I haven't heard them sing together for years, but in my dream, Mum and Aunty Les were singing again. They were perfectly harmonised and their song was a classic. "Because He lives!" What incredible words and what a wonderful song:

"Because He lives, I can face tomorrow, because He lives, all fear is gone, because I know, He holds the future, and life is worth the living just because He lives."

So that's what I now hold onto. I can't hear the song without crying. I can't sing it or I'll dissolve in tears. But, it's a lovely reminder from Jesus that despite the grief, the loss, the unanswered questions, the regrets, disappointments, the what-ifs, the what-might-have-beens and the sadness, I know that life is worth the living, just because He lives.

ABOUT THE AUTHOR

Phil grew up in Melbourne, Australia and has lived almost his entire life within 5 km of his childhood home (save for a short stint as a missionary kid in Ukarumpa, in the Highlands of Papua New Guinea). Phil is the middle of three sons of John and Judith Simpson. Phil and his brothers (Andrew and Luke) lived in a vibrant and busy household where people were highly valued. The Simpson house was rarely locked and people came and went without knocking. It was a place of welcome, respite, joy and a great deal of activity. Cars, motorbikes, go-karts, backyard cricket and acorn wars were commonplace. It was in this wonderful and joyful chaos that Phil learned many life lessons. It was a household where faith, kindness and service were lived and modelled.

After finishing school at Carey Baptist Grammar School, Phil attended Monash University and Whitley College. He was a reluctant student, but somehow managed to complete an Arts Degree, a Bachelor of Theology and a Law Degree. After a brief and unremarkable year in a commercial law firm, Phil was admitted as a Lawyer. In doing this, he joined the ranks of his two siblings and two of his uncles. He married Lara in 1996 and together they started building their own household. As newlyweds they bought an ancient VW Kombi and set off to circumnavigate Australia. This adventure set the scene for a lifetime of fun and adventure.

Phil commenced his career as a Barrister in 1999 and has been practising as an advocate ever since. He loves the freedom of working for himself and he thoroughly enjoys the human aspect of criminal advocacy. Phil and Lara have been blessed with four wonderful children. Hannah, Charlie, William and Gracie have brought so much joy and hilarity to their lives. Together they enjoy going on snow trips, beach holidays and a range of ministry related adventures.

In 2008, Phil embraced the concept of a parallel career. For 13 years he undertook his Court work while also working two days per week as a Primary School Chaplain. He spent his entire time as a Chaplain working at Blackburn Primary School in Victoria. This school was in Phil's local community and Phil thrived on the challenge of getting to know the teachers, children, parents and grand-parents. It was also the school that Phil's mum Judith attended decades earlier. During his time at Blackburn Primary School, Phil went on 27 school camps and was privileged to provide comfort and support to thousands of people during his time there. Every day brought a new challenge and adventure. Phil remains eternally grateful to the wonderful leadership that provided their unwavering support and encouragement over this time. He still enjoys a great relationship with the school and does his best to get invited back to milestone events where he enjoys great company and free food. For just about every day of his 13 years at Blackburn Primary, Phil donned a red cap. A thoughtful neighbour gave Phil a special red cap with his initial on the front. Phil wore a succession of Danny-supplied caps for years. Phil was always easy to spot as the cap was somewhat of a standout in the playground. The red cap became part of his identity and without it, he was almost unrecognisable!

Since leaving Blackburn Primary School at the end of 2020, Phil has been able to invest time and effort into a small Not-for-profit that he started with his friends. The Shed Door is a community hub space that provides a place of connection for a range of groups. In particular, it provides activities and a meeting place for youth and young adults, community organisations, men, car and bike guys, coffee lovers, prayer people, truth seekers and anyone else who happens to walk in the door. It's ad hoc, informal and profound.

Phil is always eager to connect with readers and fellow travellers. Feel free to email him at psimpson@vicbar.com.au.

Phil and Lara travel backwards and forwards to The Philippines and often take individuals and family groups with them. They love introducing people to the beauty and challenge of this wonderful place. Phil tinkers with a range of automotive projects and is besotted with his rough and ready 1956 Cadillac Coupe Deville. Phil and Lara strive to live "outside the box" and are always on the lookout for a new adventure. They continue to live in their family home that was built by Phil's grandparents in 1953.

Printed in the United States
by Baker & Taylor Publisher Services